HEALER of the HEARTCRY

Uncovering the Unconscious Work of Christ in Trauma Healing

Tricia L. Park, Ph.D., R.N.

Copyright © 2024 Tricia L. Park, Ph.D., R.N.

All rights reserved. No part of this book may be used or reproduced by any means, graphic, electronic, or mechanical, including photocopying, recording, taping or by any information storage retrieval system without the written permission of the author except in the case of brief quotations embodied in critical articles and reviews.

This book is a work of non-fiction. Unless otherwise noted, the author and the publisher make no explicit guarantees as to the accuracy of the information contained in this book and in some cases, names of people and places have been altered to protect their privacy.

WestBow Press books may be ordered through booksellers or by contacting:

WestBow Press
A Division of Thomas Nelson & Zondervan
1663 Liberty Drive
Bloomington, IN 47403
www.westbowpress.com
844-714-3454

Because of the dynamic nature of the Internet, any web addresses or links contained in this book may have changed since publication and may no longer be valid. The views expressed in this work are solely those of the author and do not necessarily reflect the views of the publisher, and the publisher hereby disclaims any responsibility for them.

Any people depicted in stock imagery provided by Getty Images are models, and such images are being used for illustrative purposes only.
Certain stock imagery © Getty Images.

This book is not a substitute for the medical advice of physicians. Readers should consult a health care professional about symptoms requiring diagnosis or attention.

Some ideas presented are concepts. They are not to be taken as absolute truth.

Case material is based upon the author's clinical work spanning 30 years. No examples presented represent any individual. Resemblance to actual persons, living or dead, is purely coincidental.

Scripture quotations are taken from the New King James Version. Copyright © 1982 by Thomas Nelson, Inc. Used by permission. All rights reserved.

ISBN: 979-8-3850-2018-8 (sc)
ISBN: 979-8-3850-2019-5 (hc)
ISBN: 979-8-3850-2020-1 (e)

Library of Congress Control Number: 2024904129

Print information available on the last page.

WestBow Press rev. date: 04/17/2024

Dedication

To God. The best heart healer I know.

TABLE OF CONTENTS

Preface ix
Introduction xi

PART 1: JOURNEY INTO THE HEART

The Heart: A Self Assessment Questionnaire xv

Chapter 1: The Spirit 1
Chapter 2: The Soul 12
Chapter 3: Distinguishing between the Human Spirit and Soul 19

PART 2: MAKING SENSE OF THE VOICES

Chapter 4: The Body's Voice 29
Chapter 5: The Soul's Voice 36
Chapter 6: The Human Spirit's Voice 43
Chapter 7: The Holy Spirit's Voice 51
Chapter 8: Other Voices 57

PART 3: HEART CONDITIONS

Chapter 9: Heart Wounds 67
Chapter 10: Heartcry 77
Chapter 11: Heart Sickness 84
Chapter 12: Heart Failure 91
Chapter 13: Heartbreak 97
Chapter 14: Heart Abuse 105
Chapter 15: Deceived Heart 111
Chapter 16: Heart–bound 117
Chapter 17: A Double Heart 123
Chapter 18: Hard Heart 129

Chapter 19: Fearful Heart	136
Chapter 20: Heart Block	142
Chapter 21: Mind–bending	148
Chapter 22: Heartworm	153
Chapter 23: Cancer of the Mind	159
Chapter 24: Cancer of the Heart	165
Chapter 25: Heart Constrictors	171
Heart Condition Screener	**179**

PART 4: HEART HEALING

Chapter 26: Christ's Work in Heart Healing	187
Chapter 27: Fostering Heart Health	196
Chapter 28: Contrite Heart	204
Chapter 29: Healthy Heartcries	210
Chapter 30: Heart Guards	215
Chapter 31: Qualities of a Healthy Heart	222
Chapter 32: Heart Worship	230
Chapter 33: Heart Song	235

Preface

A minister prayed for me once and afterward encouraged me to write. I returned to my seat, baffled. Write what? After that day, I would try to write but had few ideas and even fewer words on paper. I sensed writer's block and prayed against it. Then, I felt inspired to write about the heart. I've been a Christian and licensed clinical psychologist for almost 25 years, so writing about the soul and spirit made sense. Since God looks at (1st Samuel 16:7) and searches the heart (Jeremiah 17:10), it seemed wise to do the same.

As I began writing about the heart, I realized things amiss in my own heart. Curious and concerned, I pressed in for revelation and understanding. I realized, at times, that I would sense something with my spirit but would have trouble focusing and praying about what I picked up. The spiritual "aha moment" would fade, barely leaving a trace. I discovered various soul issues were stealing my spirit's thunder.

This book evolved from one to four sections about the heart. I started exploring the differences between the soul and spirit and tried to organize all the "voices" believers may hear. Then, one by one, I studied and outlined various heart conditions that could adversely affect a believer. As I delved deeper, I realized how many things can go wrong in the heart. I became heavy–hearted, sorting through it all. But hope was close at hand when I realized God could reveal and heal any heart condition. Realizing that believers can create or exacerbate their heart issues, I also organized and outlined steps believers can take to promote heart health.

I wrote this book to help believers differentiate between the spirit and soul and what is healthy and unhealthy heart–wise. Familiar ideas are presented along with new concepts. It's revealing and telling. This work puts into words experiences once felt but not fully understood. This book will bring comfort, counsel, clarity, and hope. I believe it will bless your heart as much as it did mine.

Introduction

Mark 16:15–18 says, "And He said to them, 'Go into all the world and preach the gospel to every creature. He who believes and is baptized will be saved; but he who does not believe will be condemned. And these signs will follow those who believe: In My name they will cast out demons; they will speak with new tongues; they will take up serpents; and if they drink anything deadly, it will by no means hurt them; they will lay hands on the sick, and they will recover.'"

Jesus gave believers the Great Commission, but why isn't it "great" for many Christians? Why do so many not minister to the lost and broken? Ignorance, complacency, and newness in the Christian walk are some reasons for the lack of fruit. But, I think deeper issues are also hindering the Body of Christ.

Believers may know that souls can fail and break. Did you know that souls can be wounded, sick, bound, split, and even suffer cancer and constriction? This book delves into overlooked and often misunderstood conditions of the heart. Psychological and spiritual concepts and relevant truth from God's Word are presented. Believers can expect to receive valuable insight into matters of the heart that will transform their lives. I am convinced that believers can be a light in the darkness after removing darkness from their hearts.

PART 1

Journey into the Heart

The Heart:
A Self Assessment Questionnaire

The following questionnaire is a self-administered tool to determine how much you know about the heart. There are no right or wrong answers. To complete the questionnaire, answer "Yes" or "No," write out your answer, or check all statements that apply. After completing the questionnaire, you will know more about your heart. Don't worry if you aren't sure about some answers. This book will fill in knowledge gaps and help you to become an expert in matters of the heart.

1. Do you know the difference between your soul and spirit? Yes No

2. Does your body have a voice? Yes No

3. What does the voice of the soul sound like?

   _____

   _____

   _____

   _____

4. Does your spirit have its own voice? Yes No

5. Would you know the difference between your spirit and the Holy Spirit? Yes No

6. What other voices contend with your own voice?
   _____ Television/radio
   _____ Work philosophy
   _____ Other people's opinions
   _____ Thoughts about hobbies, nutrition, fitness, sports, travel, etc.
   _____ Messages from the world
   _____ Social media
   _____ Commercials
   _____ Evil spirits

7. Would you know if your heart was wounded? Yes No

8. Do you know where heartcries come from? Yes No

9. Do you know what may make a person's heart sick? Yes No

10. Do you know what may make a heart fail? Yes No

11. Do you know what may break a person's heart? Yes No

12. How would you define heart abuse?

_____
_____
_____
_____

13. Would you know if your heart was deceived? Yes No

14. What does it mean if someone's heart is bound?

_____
_____
_____
_____

15. Did you know that you can have a double heart? Yes No

16. Is having a hard heart common? Yes No

17. Is having a fearful heart normal? Yes No

18. How would you describe a block in the soul?

_____
_____
_____
_____
_____

19. Can someone's soul to be radically affected by what is seen or heard? Yes No

20. Can things be taken out of a person's soul? Yes No

21. Could cancer affect the mind or heart? Yes No

22. What might constrict someone's soul?

_____
_____
_____
_____

23. How can God help bring healing to a wounded heart?

_____
_____
_____
_____

24. What can believer's do to foster heart health?

_____
_____
_____
_____
_____

25. Is it healthy to have a contrite heart? Yes No

26. Give two examples of healthy heartcries.

_____
_____
_____
_____
_____

27. List two ways to guard your heart.

_____
_____
_____
_____
_____

28. What are two qualities of a healthy heart?

_____
_____
_____
_____
_____

29. What does it mean to worship from the heart?

_____
_____
_____
_____

30. Where do heart songs originate?

_____
_____
_____
_____

CHAPTER 1

The Spirit

Now may the God of peace Himself sanctify you completely; and may your whole spirit, soul, and body be preserved blameless at the coming of our Lord Jesus Christ.
–1 Thessalonians 5:23

We are about to embark on a journey that many start but still need to finish. I'm calling it the journey into the heart. Most people associate the word "heart" with a physical (material) beating heart. The heart plays a critical role in the physical body. It pumps life–giving blood to the cells. Without a physical heart, the body would quickly die. A healthy heart is essential for life. Take care of the heart, and it will take care of you. If a person neglects the heart, it may break down. The heart needs to be understood and cared for. It requires nourishment, exercise, and rest. A person can't tax the heart too much, or it could fail.

Besides the physical heart, the word "heart" can refer to the spirit or soul. Like the physical heart, the spirit and soul require care and management. Guard the spirit and soul, and life can go well. Treat the spirit and soul carelessly, and a person can experience problems. One challenge of dealing with the spirit and soul is that they are invisible. Many don't know the difference between the spirit and the soul. This difference is foundational information. We will cover this topic first.

The Spirit is Made to Communicate with God.

The primary function of the spirit is to communicate with God. Believers talk with God, spirit (believer's spirit) to Spirit (Holy Spirit). Second Corinthians 1:21–22 says, "Now He who establishes us with you in Christ and has anointed us is God, who also has sealed us and given us the Spirit in our hearts as a guarantee." The Holy Spirit is deposited directly into believers' hearts when they trust Jesus for salvation. The Holy Spirit resides in a person's inner being. What an incredible truth. Believers become the "temple of God" (1 Corinthians 3:16: "Do you not know that you are the temple of God and that the Spirit of God dwells in you?"). After the spirit is made new, believers can talk directly to God in their hearts. He is not out there. God is within believers. By turning inward, believers can speak to God heart–to–heart.

The Holy Spirit comes upon a person in the baptism of the Holy Spirit. Acts 1:8 says, "But you shall receive power when the Holy Spirit has come upon you; and you shall be witnesses to Me in Jerusalem and in all Judea and Samaria, and to the end of the earth." A person baptized in the Holy Spirit is immersed in God. Believers can communicate with God any time. However, it can be easier to hear God after the baptism in the Holy Spirit. There is a more significant presence of God with believers after the baptism. After the apostles were baptized, the Holy Spirit began to guide them. Consider the following verses:

> While Peter thought about the vision, the Spirit said to him, "Behold, three men are seeking you. Arise therefore, go down and go with them, doubting nothing; for I have sent them." (Acts 10:19–20)

> As they ministered to the Lord and fasted, the Holy Spirit said, "Now separate to Me Barnabas and Saul for the work to which I have called them." (Acts 13:2)

> Now when they had gone through Phrygia and the region of Galatia, they were forbidden by the Holy Spirit to preach the word in Asia. (Acts 16:6)

> And finding disciples, we stayed there seven days. They told Paul through the Spirit not to go up to Jerusalem. (Acts 21:4)

> When he had come to us, he took Paul's belt, bound his own hands and feet, and said, "Thus says the Holy Spirit, 'So shall the Jews at Jerusalem bind the man who owns this belt, and deliver him into the hands of the Gentiles.'" (Acts 21:11)

While believers can communicate directly with God, He can also communicate with them. Nehemiah 2:11–12 says, "So I came to Jerusalem and was there three days. Then I arose in the night, I and a few men with me; I told no one what my God had put in my heart to do at Jerusalem; nor was there any animal with me, except the one on which I rode." This is a good example of spirit–to–Spirit communication. Notice, Nehemiah said he had something deposited in his heart from God. This is exciting. The Creator of everything put a spiritual sticky note in Nehemiah's heart. He was treasuring what he heard, and kept it to himself. Mary was also someone who treasured spiritual things in her heart. Luke 2:51 says, "Then He [Jesus] went down with them and came to Nazareth, and was subject to them, but His mother kept all these things in her heart."

The Spirit is Made to Interact with the Spirit Realm.

Just as our physical bodies interact with the natural world, the spirit interacts with the spirit realm. The story about Lazarus and the rich man reveals that people's spirits resemble their bodies. Luke 16:22–23 says, "So it was that the beggar died, and was carried by the angels to Abraham's bosom. The rich man also died and was buried. And being in torments in Hades, he lifted up his eyes and saw Abraham afar off, and Lazarus in his bosom." The rich man and Lazarus were no longer in their physical bodies. They were in the spirit realm in spiritual form. The fact that Abraham saw Lazarus in the spirit realm reveals that Lazarus's spirit looked like his physical body.

Proverbs 20:27 says, "The spirit of a man is the lamp of the Lord, searching all the inner depths of his heart." A lamp doesn't light up by itself. The human spirit is assisted by the presence of the Holy Spirit. After the Holy Spirit comes within believers, spiritual things begin to illuminate. When a person's spirit is "searching," it's looking into matters about God's kingdom. God's kingdom is a spiritual kingdom inside believer's hearts.

Luke 17:20-21 says, "Now when He [Jesus] was asked by the Pharisees when the kingdom of God would come, He answered them and said, 'The kingdom of God does not come with observation; nor will they say, See here! or See there! for indeed, the kingdom of God is within you.'" This is a foundational truth. God's kingdom is in believers' hearts. It's not what believers see with their physical eyes. God's kingdom is eternal and internal. Believers access it by the spirit.

Ecclesiastes 3:11 says, "He has made everything beautiful in its time. Also He has put eternity in their hearts, except that no one can find out the work that God does from beginning to end." "Put eternity in their hearts" means past, present, and future have been put in believers' hearts. What happened, what's happening, and what's going to happen is in the spirit realm. Believers can know things by tuning into the spirit realm.

Every believer has a part to play in God's spiritual kingdom. Believers need to know it exists and learn how to participate in it. I've attended prayer groups that started with a time of personal prayer. Afterward, people shared what they discerned in the spirit realm. It's incredible to hear the reports of what was seen and heard. In a recent meeting, one person said she became aware of what the enemy was trying to do against her job, another received instruction on how to pray about a problem, one woman received a revelation about why she was having difficulty with her cousin, and another person said she saw into the "map room" of God.

The Spirit Has Five Senses.

Just as the physical body has five senses (touch, hearing, sight, smell, and taste), a person's spirit has the same five senses. A person interacts in the spirit realm with the spiritual senses. For example, Mary and Zacharias saw angels. Most people don't go around seeing angels in the natural realm. Mary and Zacharias likely saw into the spirit realm with their spiritual eyes. Luke 1:28–29 says, "And having come in, the angel said to her, 'Rejoice, highly favored one, the Lord is with you; blessed are you among women!' But when she saw him, she was troubled at his saying, and considered what manner of greeting this was." Luke 1:11–12 says, "Then an angel of the Lord appeared to him, standing on the right side of the altar of incense. And when Zacharias saw him, he was troubled, and fear fell upon him."

Paul's conversion experience involved seeing and hearing in the spirit. Paul saw a light and heard a voice. The people around Paul listened to a voice but could not see anyone speaking. Acts 9:7 says, "And the men who journeyed with him stood speechless, hearing a voice but seeing no one." The voice came from the spirit realm. Everyone heard it with their spiritual ears. It's unclear why Paul saw a light. It may have served a spiritual purpose for Paul. (Acts 9:3–4: "As he journeyed he came near Damascus, and suddenly a light shone around him from heaven. Then he fell to the ground and heard a voice saying to him, 'Saul, Saul, why are you persecuting Me?'")

Revelation 1:10 shows John hearing in the spirit realm ("I was in the Spirit on the Lord's Day, and I heard behind me a loud voice, as of a trumpet"). Daniel saw and heard in the spirit. Daniel 10:5–9 says,

> I lifted my eyes and looked, and behold, a certain man clothed in linen, whose waist was girded with gold of Uphaz! His body was like beryl, his face like the appearance of lightning, his eyes like torches of fire, his arms and feet like burnished bronze in color, and the sound of his words like the voice of a multitude. And I, Daniel, alone saw the vision, for the men who were with me did not see the vision; but a great terror fell upon them, so that they fled to hide themselves. Therefore I was left alone when I saw this great vision, and no strength remained in me; for my vigor was turned to frailty in me, and I retained no strength. Yet I heard the sound of his words; and while I heard the sound of his words I was in a deep sleep on my face, with my face to the ground.

Spiritual experiences can affect the body and mind. The body can lose vigor. The mind can be disturbed.

Stephen saw the glory of God and Jesus in heaven. This spiritual experience was incredible. Acts 7:55 says, "But he, being full of the Holy Spirit, gazed into heaven and saw the glory of God, and Jesus standing at the right hand of God." Notice Stephen was "full of the Holy Spirit." The Holy Spirit's presence helped illuminate spiritual things. Stephen was able to gaze into heaven with his spiritual eyes.

An angel came to Joseph in a dream. Matthew 1:20 says, "But while he thought about these things, behold, an angel of the Lord appeared to him in a dream, saying, 'Joseph, son of David, do not be afraid to take to you Mary your wife, for that which is conceived in her is of the Holy Spirit.'" This passage reveals that dreams can be spiritual. It is wise to write down and pray about dream material. Dreams can contain messages from God.

There is Life in the Spirit.

Communicating with God spirit–to–Spirit and having spiritual experiences is spiritual life. Some people have a vibrant spiritual life. Others do not. Jesus beckoned people to follow Him. He never told them they had to. Believers' spiritual lives are up to them. If someone chooses to get to know God and His kingdom, that person will learn about the spiritual realm.

Just like dealing with input from the natural world can be difficult, learning to manage spiritual material can be challenging. Remember how hard it was to learn how to read? A person has to learn letters, sounds, and words. It takes time. Mathematical division also doesn't come overnight. Certain principles need to be understood first to manage the numbers. Living life in the spirit can be complicated. A believer may have a vision or a troubling dream, receive a prophecy, or sense spiritual presences. Receiving and deciphering what is received requires time and attention. Believers need to seek wisdom and understanding. Patience is needed. Growth in the spirit takes time. There is no microwaving of these processes. Complicating matters is that the body and soul's input can mask or drown out spiritual material. Therefore, believers can benefit spiritually from cultivating a peaceful mind and body.

The Spirit has Gifts.

Believers are new creations in Christ. They are baptized into the spiritual body of believers. Each believer has at least one spiritual gift. Romans 12 and 1st Corinthians 12 outline these gifts:

> Having then gifts differing according to the grace that is given to us, let us use them: If prophecy, let us prophesy in proportion to our faith; or ministry, let us use it in our ministering; he who teaches, in teaching; he who exhorts, in exhortation; he who gives, with liberality; he who leads, with diligence; he who shows mercy, with cheerfulness. (Romans 12:6–8)

> But the manifestation of the Spirit is given to each one for the profit of all: For to one is given the word of wisdom through the Spirit, to another the word of knowledge through the same Spirit, to another faith by the same Spirit, to another gifts of healings by the same Spirit, to another the working of miracles, to another prophecy, to another discerning of spirits, to another different kinds of tongues, to another interpretation of tongues. (1 Corinthians 12:7–10)

Spiritual gifts and natural talents are not the same. Natural talents coming from the Father through genetics are received at birth. Spiritual gifts are from the Holy Spirit and are received when someone is born again. People usually don't get more natural talents as they age. Christians can ask for more gifts (1 Corinthians 12:31). Someone can use natural talents anytime. Spiritual gifts operate as the Holy Spirit wills. If a Christian grieves the Holy Spirit, a spiritual gift may not work. Both Christians and nonChristians are given natural talents. Only Christians are given spiritual gifts to build up the church. A person can use both natural and spiritual gifts to glorify God.

The Spirit Has an Appetite.

A born–again spirit has an appetite. Just like the body requires food daily, the spirit needs food. The primary diet of the spirit is the Word of God. The spirit can also stay vibrant by praying in tongues, meditating on Scripture, praising/worshiping, guarding associations, and Christian fellowship (Jude 1:20: "But you, beloved, building yourselves up on your most holy faith, praying in the Holy Spirit"; and Joshua 1:8 "This book of the Law shall not depart from your mouth, but you shall meditate in it day and night, that you may observe to do according to all that is written in it. For then you will make your way prosperous, and then you will have good success."). A healthy spirit will crave spiritual things.

The Spirit is Meant to Rule Over the Soul.

Some believe the mind is the operating center, and in a way it is. But did you know that you can have a mind governed by the spirit or a mind governed by the flesh? Optimally, believers want their spirits to dictate their minds. The mind controlled by the flesh (the "carnal mind") is at war with God (Romans 8:7: "Because the carnal mind is enmity against God; for it is not subject to the law of God, nor indeed can be"). Enmity means a deep–rooted hatred or hostility. Carnally minded believers can have trouble receiving spiritual material as well as discerning God's will for their lives.

Prayer Point: Father, show me who you made me to be spiritually and give me the grace to shine my spiritual light into the world.

CHAPTER 1 KEY POINTS
The Spirit

- ❖ Besides the physical heart, the word "heart" can refer to the spirit or soul.
- ❖ Like the physical heart, the spirit and soul require care and management.
- ❖ Many don't know the difference between the spirit and soul.
- ❖ The primary function of the spirit is to communicate with God.
- ❖ Believers communicate with God spirit (believer's spirit) to Spirit (Holy Spirit).
- ❖ After the baptism in the Holy Spirit, it can be easier to hear God.
- ❖ After the apostles were baptized, the Holy Spirit began to guide them.
- ❖ The spirit is made to interact with the spirit realm.
- ❖ The human spirit is assisted by the presence of the Holy Spirit.
- ❖ When the Holy Spirit comes within believers, spiritual things begin to be illuminated.
- ❖ When a person's spirit is "searching," it is looking into matters pertaining to God's kingdom.
- ❖ Paul, John, Daniel, Stephen, and Joseph sensed things in the spirit realm.
- ❖ What happened, what's happening, and what's going to happen is in the spirit realm.
- ❖ Believers can know things by tuning into the spirit realm.
- ❖ A person interacts in the spirit realm with the spiritual senses.
- ❖ If someone chooses to get to know God and His Kingdom, that person will learn about the spiritual realm.
- ❖ Each believer has at least one spiritual gift.
- ❖ Spiritual gifts and natural talents are not the same.
- ❖ Just like the body needs food daily, the spirit also needs food.
- ❖ The primary diet of the spirit is the Word of God.
- ❖ The spirit is meant to rule over the soul.

CHAPTER 1 STUDY QUESTIONS
The Spirit

1. What is the primary function of the spirit?

2. How can the spirit interact with the spirit realm?

3. Name the 5 spiritual senses.

4. Describe Paul's experience with the spirit realm in Acts 9:7.

THE SPIRIT

5. Describe what it means to have a spiritual life.

_____

_____

_____

_____

6. What is nourishment for the spirit?

_____

_____

_____

_____

7. Is the spirit or the soul meant to rule a person?

_____

_____

_____

_____

The Soul

My soul, wait silently for God alone, for my expectation is from Him.
—Psalm 62:5

God Gave Man a Soul.

When God made man, he breathed life into him, and he became a living soul. Genesis 2:7 says, "And the Lord God formed man of the dust of the ground, and breathed into his nostrils the breath of life; and man became a living being." The Hebrew word for "being" in this verse is "nephesh," meaning mind, emotions, soul, and inner passions. It doesn't mean spirit or body. First Thessalonians 5:23 says, "Now may the God of peace Himself sanctify you completely; and may your whole spirit, soul, and body be preserved blameless at the coming of our Lord Jesus Christ." The word "soul" in this verse is "psuche" meaning the seat of emotions and will. So, we know from these passages that God provided man with a soul.

The Soul was Made to Interact With the Natural Realm.

The soul interacts with the world by the five physical senses. Input enters through the eyes, ears, nose, mouth, and skin. The mind processes sensory data and its accompanying emotional/behavioral responses. For example, a person smells chocolate chip cookies and may think of mom, childhood, and fights with siblings over who would get the first cookie. The senses take in information, and the soul processes and reacts.

The soul is distinct from the spirit and contains the mind, emotions, and will. The mind includes beliefs, thoughts, imagination, and reasoning ability. Emotions are a person's affective reaction to internal or external experiences. Feelings would be emotions felt in the body, such as heart racing with intense anger. The will has to do with how a person directs behavior. The soul is very complex. Each aspect of the soul can be healthy or disordered.

The soul also reflects a person's personality, character, and identity. Personality is a person's consistent and enduring way of thinking, feeling, and relating across situations. There are many different kinds of personalities. There are antisocial, irritable, narcissistic, and rebellious personalities. There are withdrawn, anxious, and peaceable personalities. Some aspects of a person's personality may change, but others may stay the same.

The Soul is Intimately Connected With the Spirit and Body.

The soul is like a bridge or connector between the spirit and the body. Believers need to care for the soul. When a soul has issues, the spirit can suffer. Proverbs 15:13 says, "A merry heart makes a cheerful countenance, but by sorrow of the heart the spirit is broken." In this verse, the word "heart" is "leb," meaning mind and will, and the word "spirit" is "ruah" meaning breath or spirit. If the mind breaks, the spirit can break. In my counseling practice, I've met many believers with troubled minds with little to no spiritual life. At first, this was baffling to me. These people would say they were believers but did not desire God, the Bible, church, or prayer. When I would ask about spiritual things, there was no life or energy to their responses. What was notable was that they had many problems in their souls. In light of Proverbs 15:13, it seems likely that soul issues were dampening their spiritual life.

Third John 1:2 says, "Beloved, I pray that you may prosper in all things and be in health, just as your soul prospers." The word "prospers" in this verse is "euodoo" meaning being on the right path leading to good fortune. This verse suggests that prosperity in life (e.g., relational, occupational, physical, financial, social, and spiritual well–being) depends on the soul functioning in a way that leads to success. A believer's thinking thoughts aligned with God's word, managing negative emotions, and directing behavior towards righteousness would lead to success. Believers must be mindful of the health of their souls. There are benefits to overcoming problematic issues and patterns in the soul.

Problems in the Soul Can Hinder Spiritual Growth.

The condition of the soul is critical for what believers hear and retain from God's Word. When problems arise in the mind, will, or emotions, a person's spiritual life may be adversely affected. Matthew 13:18–23 says,

> Therefore hear the parable of the sower. When anyone hears the word of the kingdom, and does not understand it, then the wicked one comes and snatches away what was sown in his heart. This is he who received seed by the wayside. But he who received the seed on stony places, this is he who hears the word and immediately receives it with joy; yet he has no root in himself, but endures only for a while. For when tribulation or persecution arises because of the word, immediately he stumbles. Now he who received seed among the thorns is he who hears the word, and the cares of this world and the deceitfulness of riches choke the word, and he becomes unfruitful. But he who received seed on the good ground is he who hears the word and understands it, who indeed bears fruit and produces: some a hundredfold, some sixty, some thirty.

When believers don't understand the Word they hear, the devil can come and take away what was received. These are wayside hearers. We could say their soul is in a rough place. A person's mind may be distracted by troubled thoughts or feelings. Some struggling in the soul may forget what they hear and not remember to pray about what they received. Believers must intentionally plant the Word in their hearts and study it out. Proverbs 4:5 admonishes, "Get wisdom! Get understanding! Do not forget, nor turn away from the words of my mouth." Notice it doesn't just say to get wisdom. Believers must seek to comprehend what they are hearing and not turn away from what they hear. Repetition helps retention and may deepen understanding as well.

Even if believers have some understanding of the Word, if they don't embrace the truth during trials, they may never see results. Soul conditions such as doubt, fear, and lukewarmness can undermine the growth of the Word of God. Believers cannot be superficial and casual in their approach to Bible study. Intentionality and focus are a must. Frivolous concerns, worldly matters, and riches cannot dominate believer's minds and hearts. All these can wreck a harvest from the Word of God. An earnest soul who can hear and understand the Word of God can reap a sizeable spiritual harvest.

The Soul Needs to Learn How to Function With the Spirit.

Early in life, the body and its instincts dictate. As children grow, their temperament and personality become more prominent. After a person is born–again, the spiritual life blossoms. The soul needs to adapt to receiving input from both the natural and spiritual realms. Many believers are used to letting their souls lead. Learning how to "walk in the Spirit" takes time, training, and experience (Galatians 5:16: "I say then: Walk in the Spirit, and you shall not fulfill the lust of the flesh."). Little by little, believers will be less mindful of things of the flesh and more aware of things transpiring in the spirit realm.

Believers need to learn to avoid interpreting spiritual material with the natural mind. Things of the spirit cannot fit into the soulish realm. First Corinthians 2:9 says, "Eye has not seen, nor ear heard, nor have entered into the heart of man the things which God has prepared for those who love Him." Man cannot conceive spiritual things with the soul. Spiritual material must be received and prayed about – not analyzed and interpreted with the mind.

Prayer Point: Father, give me insight into the landscape and workings of my soul.

CHAPTER 2 KEY POINTS
The Soul

- God provided man with a soul.
- The soul was created by God to interact with the world by the five physical senses.
- The soul is distinct from the spirit, and is comprised of the mind, emotions, and will.
- The soul reflects a person's personality, character, and identity.
- The soul is intimately connected with the spirit and body.
- The soul is like a bridge or connector between the spirit and the body.
- It is important that believers care for the soul.
- Proverbs 15:13 says, "...by sorrow of the heart the spirit is broken."
- If the mind is broken, the spirit can break.
- Prosperity in life (e.g., relational, occupational, physical, financial, social, and spiritual well–being) depends on the soul functioning in a way that leads to success.
- The condition of the soul is critical for what believers hear and retain from God's Word.
- Believers must intentionally plant the Word in their hearts and study it out.
- Soul conditions such as doubt, fear, and lukewarmness can undermine the growth of the Word of God.
- An earnest soul who can hear and understand the Word of God can reap a sizeable spiritual harvest.
- The soul needs to learn how to function with the spirit.
- Many believers are used to letting their soul lead.
- After being born–again, the soul needs to get used to receiving input from both the natural and spiritual realms.
- Man cannot conceive spiritual things with the soul.
- Spiritual material must be received and prayed about – not analyzed and interpreted with the mind.

CHAPTER 2 STUDY QUESTIONS
The Soul

1. Write out a Scripture showing that God gave man a soul.

   _____
   _____
   _____
   _____

2. How does the soul interact with the world?

   _____
   _____
   _____
   _____

3. The soul is comprised of which of the following? (check all that apply)
   ___ Intellect
   ___ Reason
   ___ Imagination
   ___ Emotions
   ___ Feelings
   ___ Will
   ___ Hunger
   ___ Personality
   ___ Character
   ___ Identity

4. The soul is like a _____ or _____ between the spirit and body.

5. Give one example of how a soul issue could affect a person's spiritual life.

_____
_____
_____
_____

6. Describe how the soul can work with the spirit.

_____
_____
_____
_____

7. Should spiritual material be interpreted with the natural mind? Yes No

CHAPTER 3

Distinguishing between the Human Spirit and Soul

For the word of God is living and powerful, and sharper than any two-edged sword, piercing even to the division of soul and spirit, and of joints and marrow, and is a discerner of the thoughts and intents of the heart.
—Hebrews 4:12

Chapters 1 and 2 outlined attributes of the spirit and soul. These two parts of the inner person are distinct and have unique properties and purposes. Differentiating between the spirit and soul can be challenging. While one could argue that both the spirit and soul are "you," I would suggest that one is the "true you" and the other is the "changeable you."

The "True You" is the Born-Again Spirit.

Believers' born-again spirits are who God made them to be. The Bible teaches that "God is Spirit"(John 4:24). Believers' spirits are born from God. John 3:6–8 says, "That which is born of the flesh is flesh, and that which is born of the Spirit is spirit. Do not marvel that I say to you, 'You must be born again.' The wind blows where it wishes, and you hear the sound of it, but cannot tell where it comes from and where it goes. So is everyone who is born of the Spirit." Believers are God's offspring. They are spirits with unique gifts and talents. One believer may see in the spirit often. Another believer may not see in the spirit but experiences an incredible unction to lay hands on sick people. Another believer may get revelations about the Bible. Still, another believer may feel compelled to preach the gospel. These are examples of the "true you"/spiritual part of believers.

The "Changeable" Part of the Person is the Soul.

The soul is changeable because the contents and health of the soul can vary widely over time. As a psychologist, I see this often. I may meet a person and work with that individual for a year. I may meet with the same person five years later and feel like I don't recognize them psychologically. How a person thinks, feels, and behaves can change over time. I've met depressed, anxious, and isolated people who later were happy, peaceful, and gainfully employed. I'm not saying all parts of the soul change with age, but many do.

A Person's Spirit Will Possess More Attributes of God than the Soul.

Spiritually, believers are new creations in Christ. Second Corinthians 5:17 says, "Therefore, if anyone is in Christ, he is a new creation; old things have passed away; behold, all things have become new." The spirit is made new at the time of salvation. The soul remains the same after the new birth. The Bible teaches that believers can have spiritual abilities like God. John 14:12 says, "Most assuredly, I say to you, he who believes in Me, the works that I do he will do also; and greater works than these he will do, because I go to My Father." Believers can also do things that nonbelievers can't do. Mark 15:17–18 says, "And these signs will follow those who believe: In My name they will cast out demons; they will speak with new tongues; they will take up serpents; and if they drink anything deadly, it will be no means hurt them; they will lay hands on the sick, and they will recover."

The Spirit and Soul Contain Different Material.

Spiritual things are mysterious. I entered my home once, looked outside, and saw a figure floating near my window. The figure appeared to be a woman with long hair in a dress. I was speechless. My soul had been thinking about eating a snack. My spirit began to pray. I would have never imagined I would see a spectre with my eyes. God allowed me to glimpse into the spirit realm. The experience had a purpose, and I grew spiritually by pressing into the matter.

Another time, I came home from church and noticed a man sitting in a car in front of my apartment. I had seen the car every day for four days. I thought it odd because I had never seen it before. After stepping into my apartment, I had a spiritual vision of a headline from the newspaper that day, "Woman kidnapped." I also saw a flash of a video clip about a kidnapping. I said, "Lord, why am I seeing these images?" He said, "The man out front is here to kidnap you." I stared blankly for a few seconds. Then I got mad. I said, "No way. I've got things to do." I asked God what to do. He said, "Praise Me." I praised God for a few minutes while pacing back and forth. When I peeked out the window, the car was gone. I never saw the man again. Thank goodness I paid attention to what I saw and heard in the spirit. God warned me and saved me. In perilous times, we especially need to hear from God.

Isaiah 55:8–9 says, "For My thoughts are not your thoughts, nor are your ways My ways," says the LORD. For as the heavens are higher than the earth, so are My ways higher than your ways, and My thoughts than your thoughts." When believers receive a message from God, they usually know it. I was in prayer once and heard, "Possess your possession." This phrase was foreign to me. I immediately started praying and received understanding from the Holy Spirit. Without seeking God, I may have never known what that phrase meant at that season of my life. When believers immerse themselves in the Kingdom of God, they will learn how God speaks and the language He uses.

The soul contains material related to the senses and experiences. With the mind, people may think about their neighbors as they drive by their houses, ponder fond memories, solve a problem, or imagine something new in their future. With the soul, a person may try to figure out why they feel fear or anger. Decisions about behavior can also come from the soul. Someone may be upset by a person's word choice and decide to leave the room. A person may think about spiritual material such as a prophecy received. Still, it would be with the soul's faculties, not the spirit.

The Word of God Helps Distinguish Between the Spirit and Soul.

Hebrews 4:12 says, "For the word of God is living and powerful, and sharper than any two-edged sword, piercing even to the division of soul and spirit, and of joints and marrow, and is a discerner of the thoughts and intents of the heart." The word "soul" in this verse is "psuche" meaning a person's distinct identity or personality. The word "spirit" is "pneuma" meaning wind or breath. The Word of God helps differentiate between soulish and spiritual ideas. For example, say a believer gets two ideas while praying. One idea is to play music for nursing home residents on their birthday, and the other is to travel thru France on a sightseeing tour. Scripture would suggest that the first idea was from the spirit (James 1:27: "Pure and undefiled religion before God and the Father is this: to visit orphans and widows in their trouble, and to keep oneself unspotted from the world."). The second idea seems soulish since it focuses on the self rather than others. When believers receive an idea from God, it tends to align with His Word.

    A notable difference between the spirit and soul is that the spirit is automatically renewed daily (2nd Corinthians 4:16: "Therefore we do not lose heart. Even though our outward man is perishing, yet the inward man is being renewed day by day"). The word "renewed" in this verse is "anakainoo," meaning going from one stage to a higher level. The spirit is progressing each day. The soul may not get better each day. In fact, it may become more disordered. Renewal of the soul is not automatic.

    Prayer Point: Father, help me understand the differences between my spirit and soul and manage them properly.

CHAPTER 3 KEY POINTS
Distinguishing between the Human Spirit and Soul

- Differentiating between the spirit and soul can be challenging.
- The "true you" is the born-again spirit.
- Believers' born-again spirits are who God made them to be.
- Believers spirits are born from God.
- The "changeable" part of the person is the soul.
- The contents and health of the soul can change over time.
- Spiritually, believers are new creations in Christ.
- The soul remains the same after the new birth.
- Believers can have spiritual abilities like God.
- Believers can also do things that nonbelievers can't do.
- The spirit and soul contain different material.
- The things of the spirit are mysterious; the mind can't imagine them.
- The Word of God helps differentiate between soulish and spiritual ideas.
- When believers receive an idea from God, it tends to align with His Word.
- A notable difference between the spirit and soul is that the spirit is automatically renewed daily.
- Renewal of the soul is not automatic.

CHAPTER 3 STUDY QUESTIONS
Distinguishing between the Human Spirit and Soul

1. What makes a person's spirit unique from the soul after the new birth?

2. Does the soul change at the time of the new birth? Yes No

3. What makes the soul changeable?

4. Name two God–like attributes of a person's spirit.

5. Describe one thing a believer can do that a nonbeliever cannot do.

6. How can the Word of God help distinguish between the spirit and soul?

_____
_____
_____
_____

7. Is the soul automatically renewed daily? Yes No

PART 2

Making Sense of the Voices

CHAPTER 4

The Body's Voice

But put on the Lord Jesus Christ, and make no provision for the flesh, to fulfill its lusts.
—Romans 13:14

Each part of our being has a voice, a language, a way of communicating. Making sense of these voices is critical for believers. The first voice people become aware of is the body's voice. Infants become aware of the body's voice around mealtimes. The body signals the need for food and water. The infant communicates hunger and thirst by crying, rooting against the mother, or becoming irritable. Children discern other bodily voices such as temperature, fullness, pressure, and pain. People must attend to the body's voices.

Consider someone with ankle pain. Maybe there was an injury or excessive use. If that person heeds the pain signals, slowing down, resting, and icing the area may foster healing. If a person ignores the pain, the ankle issue may worsen. With ongoing use, what started as a painful area may become broken and unusable.

The body of someone with diabetes has a way of communicating. High and low blood sugars usher in symptoms including thirst and excessive hunger. Attention to diabetic symptoms helps a person manage the condition. Ignoring signs could contribute to adverse short and long-term effects, including lethargy, confusion, and neuropathy. It benefits people to listen to their bodies.

The Old Man.

Ephesians 4:22 says, "That you put off, concerning your former conduct, the old man which grows corrupt according to the deceitful lusts." The old man is the nature of man before conversion and regeneration. It's the inherited sin nature which manifests through the soul and body. The old man may want to drink excessively, swear, and lie. The old man acts out through the body and soul because these remain unregenerate after the new birth. The old man and the accompanying sins must be rendered dead by the power of the Holy Spirit. (Romans 8:13: "For if you live according to the flesh you will die; but if by the Spirit you put to death the deeds of the body, you will live.")

Matthew 26:41 says, "Watch and pray, lest you enter into temptation. The spirit indeed is willing, but the flesh is weak." The word "weak" in this verse is "asthenes," meaning without strength and vigor. Due to its frail nature, the flesh can easily give in to the desires of the sinful nature. For example, Jesus gave his disciples a directive to watch while He prayed one night. When Jesus returned to check on them, they had all fallen asleep. Jesus was merciful and explained why they failed. Their spirits likely wanted to obey God, but their souls and bodies (afflicted by sorrow and fatigue) gave in to the urge to sleep.

No matter how strong a believer's spirit may be, the old man may resurrect. The soul and body briefly take over when the old man surfaces and believers may sin. Such missteps are not uncommon. Importantly, believers must confess the sin and be determined to walk in their righteousness in Christ (2nd Corinthians 5:21). For example, a believer may get frustrated by mistreatment at work. That person may give in to the old sinful nature, kick a garbage can, and rage at someone. The unloving behavior would need to be confessed. Instead of letting the old man take over, a believer could inwardly say, "I feel furious about something right now, but I'm going to process the matter before I talk to anyone." Believers must reign over the flesh's desires.

Believers can be unchristlike at times. Fortunately, believers are not their behavior. They are beautiful spirits learning to put the body and soul under the Lordship of Jesus. Putting the flesh under can be challenging. Along with pushing down the old man, is putting on the "new man." Colossians 3:9–10 says, "Do not lie to one another, since you have put off the old man with his deeds, and have put on the new man who is renewed in knowledge according to the image of Him who created him." Donning the new man is allowing God to be visible on the outside. Putting on the armor of God is like putting on God. Ephesians 6:14–18 says,

> Stand therefore, having girded your waist with truth, having put on the breastplate of righteousness, and having shod your feet with the preparation of the gospel of peace; above all, taking the shield of faith with which you will be able to quench all the fiery darts of the wicked one. And take the helmet of salvation, and the sword of the Spirit, which is the word of God; praying always with all prayer and supplication in the Spirit, being watchful to this end with all perseverance and supplication for all the saints.

Psalm 73:26 says, "My flesh and my heart fail; but God is the strength of my heart and my portion forever." When believers miss the mark and sin, they can rely on God to help them recover and sustain them. Believers must remember that they are alive in Christ now. Believers previously acted like the world. Now, they follow and imitate Jesus. It's a significant shift. It takes time to work out what God put on the inside. Ephesians 2:1–3 says, "And you He made alive, who were dead in trespasses and sins, in which you once walked according to the course of this world, according to the prince of the power of the air, the spirit who now works in the sons of disobedience, among whom also we all once conducted ourselves in the lusts of our flesh, fulfilling the desires of the flesh and of the mind, and were by nature children of wrath, just as the others." Before salvation, believers were followers of the world's ways. After salvation, believers learn to follow God's ways.

Aim for a Sanctified body.

Sanctify means to set apart for God's purposes. Aim to set apart the body for spiritual service (e.g., prayer, praise, scripture meditation, worship, preaching, teaching, laying hands on the sick, and casting out demons). To do that, believers must rule over their bodies. Bodily discipline is a must for God's servants. First Corinthians 9:27 says, "But I discipline my body and bring it into subjection, lest, when I have preached to others, I myself should become disqualified." A sanctified body has been trained to do what the spirit dictates. Philippians 3:19 says, "Whose end is destruction, whose god is their belly, and whose glory is in their shame – who set their mind on earthly things." If a believer's appetite is in control, that person is likely operating from the flesh rather than the spirit.

Godliness is more important than physical exercise. First Timothy 4:8 says, "For bodily exercise profits a little, but godliness is profitable for all things, having promise of the life that now is and of that which is to come." Physical exercise has a small payout. When believers focus on things of the spirit, there are widespread benefits now and later.

Prayer Point: Father, thank you for a wondrous physical body. Help me to take care of it, and to bring it under the rule of my spirit.

CHAPTER 4 KEY POINTS
The Body's Voice

- ❖ Each part of our being has a voice, a language, a way of communicating.
- ❖ Infants become aware of the body's voice around mealtimes.
- ❖ Children discern other bodily voices such as temperature, fullness, pressure, and pain.
- ❖ It's important that people become aware and attend to the body's voices.
- ❖ The old man is the nature of man before conversion and regeneration.
- ❖ The old man acts out through the body and soul because these remain unregenerate after the new birth.
- ❖ Due to its frail nature, the flesh can easily give in to the desires of the sin nature.
- ❖ No matter how strong a Christian's spirit may be, the old man may resurrect.
- ❖ Believers must be careful not to let the flesh rule; the spirit was meant to reign.
- ❖ Along with putting off the old man is the task of putting on the "new man."
- ❖ Aim to set apart the body for spiritual services (e.g., prayer, praise, scripture meditation, worship, preaching, teaching, laying hands on the sick, and casting out demons).
- ❖ Bodily discipline is a must for God's servants.
- ❖ A sanctified body has been trained to do what the spirit dictates.
- ❖ Godliness is more important than physical exercise.

CHAPTER 4 STUDY QUESTIONS
The Body's Voice

---

1. Name three voices of the body.

2. What is the old man?

3. Why can the old man resurrect?

4. Is the flesh strong? Yes No

5. How could a person put on the new man?

6. What is a sanctified body?

_____
_____
_____
_____

7. Is physical exercise more important than spiritual practices?

_____
_____
_____
_____

CHAPTER 5

The Soul's Voice

My soul thirsts for God, for the living God.
When shall I come and appear before God?
—Psalm 42:2

The soul consists of the mind (thoughts, beliefs, imaginations, intellect, and reasoning), emotions (moods and affect), will (directed behavior), and personality (enduring ways of thinking, feeling, and relating in the world). Each person's soul is unique. Just as the body has a voice, the soul has a voice. The soul interacts with the outer world through the senses. Thus, the voice of the soul often sounds like the world. It will contain beliefs, ideas, attitudes, thoughts, and emotions based on worldly experiences. Born–again believers also may have thoughts and feelings about spiritual material (e.g., the Bible, prophecies, revelations) in their souls.

Souls are incredibly complicated. There are many facets and dimensions to the soul. I liken the soul to a large garden. People usually select what they want in their gardens. However, some things get in unknowingly (e.g., weeds, chipmunk holes, debris, deer droppings). Experiences get planted in the soul. Positive experiences get intentionally placed. Negative experiences such as trauma, abuse, and neglect get in without permission. People's upbringing often set up enduring features in the soul, including expectations, values, preferences, and behavioral patterns. For example, one person may always get out bed before sunrise and think people are "lazy" if they don't rise early. Some people may think arguing is a typical way of communicating because that's what they experienced in childhood. Each soul is distinct in its perspectives and history.

Soul Management.

To cultivate a healthy soul, people must first take inventory. They need to identify what is in their soul and organize it. Uprooting negative thoughts and beliefs is a must. A healthy mindset will align with God's Word. For example, believing one can get through a custody battle with God's assistance would be healthy. Thoughts such as, "Things will never get better" or "No one cares about what I am going through" would be unhealthy. Management of the mind is critical for optimum mental health.

Speaking to the soul is a healthy mind management strategy. Psalm 42:11 says, "Why are you cast down, O my soul? And why are you disquieted within me? Hope in God; For I shall yet praise Him, the help of my countenance and my God." Relying on God is another way to manage the soul in stressful times. Psalm 50:15 says, "Call upon Me in the day of trouble; I will deliver you, and you shall glorify Me." Believers are never alone. When calamity strikes, God is ready with His divine assistance. All believers have to do is ask. It can make a world of difference for the soul.

First Peter 2:25 says, "For you were like sheep going astray, but have now returned to the Shepherd and Overseer of your souls." God wants to be the leader, feeder, and supervisor of people's souls. He knows how to guide and repair wounded and failing souls. Believers can trust God with their souls. Ezekiel 18:4 says, "Behold, all souls are Mine; The soul of the father as well as the soul of the son is Mine; The soul who sins shall die." God creates all souls and never gives up ownership. If people pull away from God, there can be a high cost. Thankfully, from birth to death, God willingly takes care of souls. Isaiah 41:10 says, "Fear not, for I am with you; Be not dismayed, for I am your God. I will strengthen you, Yes, I will help you, I will uphold you with My righteous right hand." We have a standby God. He is only far if we leave Him.

Soul management has benefits now and later. Matthew 16:26 says, "For what profit is it to a man if he gains the whole world, and loses his own soul? Or what will a man give in exchange for his soul?" The word "loses" in this verse is "zemioo," meaning to cause to experience loss with penalty; forfeiture. God created all people and invites them to get to know Him and follow His ways. If believers focus on earthly treasures, it will be at the cost of their souls. Souls can break down and fail. Thankfully, God can restore souls. Psalm 23:3 says, "He restores my soul; He leads me in the paths of righteousness for His name's sake." God can bring wholeness and vitality back to souls.

The Mind of Christ.

First Corinthians 2:16 says, "For 'who has known the mind of the Lord that he may instruct Him?' But we have the mind of Christ." The mind of Christ isn't the mind of Jesus. "Christ" means "anointed." It's saying let the mind of the "anointed" be in you. When something is anointed, it is enabled and facilitated. Not everyone who serves God is anointed. David (1st Samuel 16:13), Saul (1st Samuel 10:1), Jehu (2nd Kings 9:3), and Solomon (1st Kings 1:34) were "anointed."

Jesus also received the mind of the anointed. A person with the mind of Christ has different words and ways of speaking. They have entered into the consciousness of the anointed. They are operating like beings functioning with information from Father God Himself. Philippians 2:5 says, "Let this mind be in you which was also in Christ Jesus." The Father empowered Jesus' mind. It greatly benefits believers to seek God for divine assistance in their thinking.

Renewing the Mind.

Romans 12:2 says, "And do not be conformed to this world, but be transformed by the renewing of your mind, that you may prove what is that good and acceptable and perfect will of God." Renewing the mind does not give a person the mind of Christ. In mind renewal, a believer replaces old information with Biblical information. For example, some do not believe God heals. The Bible says that God is our healer in the Old and New Testaments (Exodus 15:26; Isaiah 53:5; Matthew 12:15). After mind renewal, what a person says and does aligns with the Word of God. Some people resist God because their mind is unrenewed.

Aim for a Sanctified Mind.

A sanctified mind focuses on God's thoughts and purposes. It isn't full of worldly ideas. It purposes to think about God's priorities. It aims to embrace all God has said about who they are in Christ.

Prayer Point: Father, thank you for giving me a beautiful soul. Help me to manage it wisely and to sanctify it with Your Word.

CHAPTER 5 KEY POINTS
The Soul's Voice

- ❖ The soul consists of the mind (thoughts, intellect, reasoning, beliefs), emotions (moods and affect), will (directed behavior), and personality (temperament and enduring ways of thinking, feeling, and relating in the world).
- ❖ Just as the body has a voice, the soul has a voice.
- ❖ The voice of the soul often sounds like the world.
- ❖ Born–again believers also may have thoughts and feelings about spiritual experiences in their souls.
- ❖ The are many facets and dimensions to the soul.
- ❖ The soul is like a large garden.
- ❖ In people's souls, things get intentionally and unintentionally planted.
- ❖ People's upbringing often set up enduring features in the soul, including expectations, values, preferences, and behavioral patterns.
- ❖ To cultivate a healthy soul, people must first take inventory. They need to identify what is in their soul and organize it.
- ❖ Uprooting negative thoughts and beliefs is a must.
- ❖ Speaking to the soul is a healthy mind management strategy.
- ❖ Relying on God is another way to manage the soul in stressful times.
- ❖ God wants to be the leader, feeder, and supervisor of people's souls.
- ❖ Soul management has benefits now and later.
- ❖ Souls can break down and fail. Thankfully, God can restore souls.
- ❖ A person who receives the mind of Christ has different words and ways of speaking.
- ❖ In mind renewal, a believer replaces old information with Biblical information.
- ❖ A sanctified mind focuses on God's thoughts and purposes.

CHAPTER 5 STUDY QUESTIONS
The Soul's Voice

---

1. Describe different aspects of the soul.

2. What does the soul's voice sound like?

3. What have you intentionally planted in your soul?

4. What has been unintentionally planted in your soul?

5. List two healthy thoughts you have regularly.

_____
_____
_____
_____

6. Is it Biblical to speak to your soul? Yes No

7. Can a believer restore their soul with mind renewal? Yes No

8. Describe the mind of Christ?

_____
_____
_____
_____

9. What does it mean when someone's mind is renewed?

_____
_____
_____
_____

CHAPTER 6

The Human Spirit's Voice

For what man knows the things of a man except the spirit of the man which is in him? Even so no one knows the things of God except the Spirit of God.
—1 Corinthians 2:11

Just as the body and soul have a voice, the human spirit has a voice. The spirit's voice is the "inner voice." It's deep within a person. It's not based on sensory information from the world. The human spirit's voice is based upon spiritual material because of its connection to the Holy Spirit and the spirit realm.

A person's spirit will not be thinking about a plate of lasagna and garlic bread. That idea would come from thoughts based on sensory experiences. One's spirit is going to be pondering spiritual things. Things of the spirit are usually above and beyond the natural reality. They can be hard to fit into the soulish realm and language.

The spirit's voice may be felt as an unction or leading in the gut. For example, Tom recalled feeling like he had to pray for Samantha one day. Tom was busy working at the time. Deep down, he felt like his spirit yelled, "Pray!" Tom later found out Samantha was in a car accident when he felt compelled to pray. Tom already knew her husband had been diagnosed with cancer the week before. His spirit (connected to the Holy Spirit) sensed he needed to pray. It's good that Tom heeded the unction since Samantha was in intense distress.

I felt led to drive to a chapel a few hours away once. Going so far didn't make logical sense, but my spirit kept prompting me to go. I had previously prayed for a young man there a few times. I texted him several times before I arrived. He usually responded within minutes. I even left a voicemail. Still no reply. Late that night, a friend told me the young man committed suicide that day. I was shocked. In prayer, I realized God was trying to help the man by sending me to his chapel, but he chose to ignore the messages.

The Born Again Spirit's Voice.

An anthem of the born–again spirit is, "What can I do for you?" It's like a song continually playing in believers' hearts. When there is a need, the born–again spirit will feel it and want to do something. I remember when God started teaching me about my spirit's voice. I was struggling to work in nursing homes as a psychologist. There was so much need. I often felt overwhelmed. Burnout and exhaustion got worse during COVID–19. Life started feeling heavy and dark. My spirit started crying, "I know You, Father. You can do all things. Help these people more!" I realized this was my spirit's voice because it was related to spiritual understanding. In contrast, my soul was saying, "These situations are hopeless." On the outside, things were dismal. Stage 4 cancers, kidney failures, strokes, broken hips and hearts. Inwardly, I knew that the Creator of all things could turn every terrible situation around.

Another powerful sentiment of believers' spirits is, "God is for you, not against you." It's life–transforming when people learn that Jesus' sacrifice brought peace between God and man. We've all sinned many times, so many feel bad and may not think to talk to God. While the soul and body may not want to share the gospel, the born–again spirit does. The born-again spirit is connected to God, and God wants everyone to know that the sin problem has been eliminated. We are in the age of grace. It is a time of reconciliation with God. God is waiting with open arms for people to come to Him. God is relying on His church to tell all people the good news.

The Language of Love.

Take a minute and answer 'Yes' or 'No' to the following questions. Have you ever:

Yes No Felt uncomfortable after complaining about a neighbor?
Yes No Felt bad after snapping at someone for no apparent reason?
Yes No Become upset when a new employee received a raise and you didn't?
Yes No Felt uneasy talking about an award?
Yes No Experienced a loss of peace after acting rude or self–centered?

The statements above reflect situations in which someone was unloving (e.g., complaining, snapping, envying, bragging, and being rude or self–centered). Love is believers' standard and measuring line. It is the language of believers' hearts. If believers go against love, they can feel out of sorts. First Corinthians 13:4–8 says,

> Love suffers long and is kind; love does not envy; love does not parade itself; is not puffed up; does not behave rudely, does not seek its own, is not provoked, thinks no evil; does not rejoice in iniquity but rejoices in the truth; bears all things, believes all things, hopes all things, endure all things. Love never fails. But whether there are prophecies they will fail; whether there are tongues, they will cease; whether there is knowledge, it will vanish away.

The next time you feel a loss of peace, check if your behavior has been unloving.

The Voice of Spiritual Understanding.

Spiritual understanding is the unique insight and comprehension of a believer's spirit. Colossians 1:9 says, "For this reason we also, since the day we heard it, do not cease to pray for you, and to ask that you may be filled with the knowledge of His will in all wisdom and spiritual understanding." Knowing to pray for enemies rather than hating them and abstaining from lying would be spiritual understanding. Having spiritual understanding is associated with knowing God's will.

Consider the Exodus. Here are people living in the world who start having supernatural experiences. God led the children of Israel out of Egypt to go to the Promised Land. While they had a destination, they lacked understanding of God's will. They were only beginning to learn about God's ways. They didn't know their life had a spiritual purpose. They only saw themselves as coming out of Egypt. The people of Israel kept doing what they knew naturally. When Moses went up the mountain to receive the Ten Commandments, he was gone for 40 days and nights. In his absence, the Israelites made a golden calf to worship. This idea probably came from what they knew in Egypt. They lacked spiritual understanding and were not familiar with God's ways.

In contrast, Jesus focused on doing the Father's will. He had a spiritual understanding of God the Father. John 4:34 says, "Jesus said to them, 'My food is to do the will of Him who sent Me, and to finish His work.'" Completing the Father's will motivated and sustained Jesus. Believers need to discern the Father's will. In John 8:29, Jesus said, "And He who sent Me is with Me. The Father has not left Me alone, for I always do those things that please Him." Not knowing the Father's will can lead to doing "good things" rather than "God things." Believers must pray and strive to walk with God.

Praying with Spiritual Understanding.

First Corinthians 14:14–15 says, "For if I pray in a tongue, my spirit prays, but my understanding is unfruitful. What is the conclusion then? I will pray with the spirit, and I will also pray with the understanding. I will sing with the spirit, and I will also sing with the understanding." Praying with understanding can be basing a prayer upon spiritual or sensory data. For example, a believer may know that someone has lung cancer. That is natural information. Knowing that it is God's will to heal is spiritual understanding. Furthermore, the Holy Spirit may reveal that the person has unforgiveness and bitterness. With natural and spiritual understanding, a believer could effectively pray for healing of cancer, unforgiveness, and bitterness.

Prayer Point: Father, help me discern my spirit's voice, follow the flow of love, and gain spiritual understanding.

CHAPTER 6 KEY POINTS
The Human Spirit's Voice

- ❖ The spirit's voice is the "inner voice." It's deep within a person.
- ❖ The human spirit's voice is based upon spiritual material because of its connection to the Holy Spirit and the spirit realm.
- ❖ Things of the spirit are usually above and beyond the natural reality.
- ❖ The spirit's voice may be felt as an unction or leading in the gut.
- ❖ An anthem of the born again spirit is, "What can I do for you?"
- ❖ Another powerful sentiment of believers' spirits is, "God is for you, not against you."
- ❖ It's life–transforming when people learn that Jesus' sacrifice brought peace between God and man.
- ❖ Love is believers' standard and measuring line. It is the language of believers' hearts.
- ❖ If believers go against love, they can feel out of sorts.
- ❖ Spiritual understanding is the unique insight and comprehension of a believer's spirit.
- ❖ Having spiritual understanding is associated with knowing God's will.
- ❖ Praying with understanding can be basing a prayer upon spiritual or sensory data.

CHAPTER STUDY 6 QUESTIONS
The Human Spirit's Voice

---

1. What does the human spirit's voice sound like?

   _____
   _____
   _____
   _____

2. Name two ways you may sense the human spirit's voice?

   _____
   _____
   _____
   _____

3. What are two anthem's of the born–again spirit?

   _____
   _____
   _____
   _____

4. What could cause a believer to feel out of sorts?

   _____
   _____
   _____
   _____

5. Define spiritual understanding.
_____
_____
_____
_____

6. Describe how praying with spiritual understanding can be helpful.
_____
_____
_____
_____

CHAPTER

The Holy Spirit's Voice

But when they arrest you and deliver you up, do not worry beforehand, or premeditate what you will speak. But whatever is given you in that hour, speak that; for it is not you who speak, but the Holy Spirit.
– Mark 13:11

Prophesying is speaking from the inspiration of the Holy Spirit. Second Peter 1:21 says, "For prophecy never came by the will of man, but holy men of God spoke as they were moved by the Holy Spirit." When believers prophesy, the Holy Spirit forms the message. Prophecy is one voice of the Holy Spirit thru believers. The unsaved can also prophesy because the Holy Spirit is upon all flesh. Joel 2:28 says, "And it shall come to pass afterward that I will pour out My Spirit on all flesh; Your sons and your daughters shall prophesy, your old men shall dream dreams, your young men shall see visions. And also on My menservants and on My maidservants I will pour out My Spirit in those days."

I became very thirsty prayer walking once. I ended up at a gas station miles away from my starting point, but had no money. A stranger came over and offered me a drink. We talked briefly, and I learned he had no faith in God. However, some of the things he said sounded so spiritual. I was stunned. I asked God what happened. He indicated that the man had prophesied because the Holy Spirit was upon him.

Another outstanding way the Holy Spirit speaks through a person is when they speak in tongues. Acts 2:3–4 says, "Then there appeared to them divided tongues, as of fire, and one sat upon each of them. And they were all filled with the Holy Spirit and began to speak with other tongues, as the Spirit gave them utterance." Speaking in tongues is a sign that a believer has been baptized in the Holy Spirit. Acts 19:5–6 says, "When they heard this they were baptized in the name of the Lord Jesus. And when Paul had laid hands on them, the Holy Spirit came upon them, and they spoke with tongues and prophesied." Speaking in tongues and prophesying are amazing signs that the Holy Spirit is working through believers.

The Holy Spirit's voice also can be discerned by what He does. In the Scriptures, the Holy Spirit is: Teacher, Helper, Intercessor, Standby, Sanctifier, Advocate, Comforter, and Counselor. Consider the following Scriptures:

> **Teacher.** But the Helper, the Holy Spirit, whom the Father will send in My name, He will teach you all things, and bring to your remembrance all things that I said to you. (John 14:26)
>
> **Helper.** And I will pray the Father, and He will give you another Helper, that He may abide with you forever. (John 14:16)
>
> **Intercessor.** Likewise the Spirit also helps in our weaknesses. For we do not know what we should pray for as we ought, but the Spirit Himself makes intercession for us with groanings which cannot be uttered. Now He who searches the hearts knows what the mind of the Spirit is, because He makes intercession for the saints according to the will of God. (Romans 8:26–28)
>
> **Standby and Advocate.** But the Helper (Comforter, Advocate, Intercessor – Counselor, Strengthener, Standby), the Holy Spirit, whom the Father will send in My name

[in My place, to represent Me and act on My behalf], He will teach you all things. And He will help you remember everything that I have told you. (John 14:26 Amplified version)

Sanctifier. Peter, an apostle of Jesus Christ, to the pilgrims of the Dispersion in Pontus, Galatia, Cappadocia, Asia, and Bithynia, elect according to the foreknowledge of God the Father, in sanctification of the Spirit, for obedience and sprinkling of the blood of Jesus Christ: Grace to you and peace be multiplied. (1 Peter 1:1–2)

Comforter. Then the churches throughout all Judea, Galilee, and Samaria had peace and were edified. And walking in the fear of the Lord and in the comfort of the Holy Spirit, they were multiplied. (Acts 9:31)

Counselor. For what man knows the things of a man except the spirit of the man which is in him? Even so no one knows the things of God except the Spirit of God. (1 Corinthians 2:11)

Someone speaking by the Holy Spirit may speak boldly and powerfully. Acts 1:8 says, "But you shall receive power when the Holy Spirit has come upon you; and you shall be witnesses to Me in Jerusalem, and in all Judea and Samaria, and to the end of the earth." When the Holy Spirit is upon believers, a message about Jesus can at times easily flow out. I met a street preacher testifying about Jesus once who I could hear two blocks away. This was amazing because he was preaching without a microphone.

When led by the Holy Spirit, a believer may do something out of the ordinary. I saw a woman in a parking lot once. The Holy Spirit encouraged me to pray for her. I didn't know her, so I hesitated. I said, "If she walks out of this store when I do, I will pray for her." Guess what? The woman walked out when I did. I went to her and told her God prompted me to come over and pray for her. Through tears, she said she had a brain tumor. God knew about her turmoil and wanted to comfort her. I shared words of encouragement and prayed for her healing. She was so grateful. What a privilege believers have of working with God to help people.

The Holy Spirit may bring to remembrance something a person hasn't thought about in years. Maybe it's a story, experience, or testimony. Believers need to share what comes to their hearts. God wants to help people. He may use believers' life experiences to build up another person.

John 15:26 says, "But when the Helper comes, whom I [Jesus] shall send to you from the Father, the Spirit of truth who proceeds from the Father, He will testify of Me." If a believer's words do not glorify the Lord Jesus, the message may not be from the Holy Spirit. Believers can pray for the gift of discernment to help differentiate between a human spirit, the Holy Spirit, and an evil spirit (1 Corinthians 12:10). First Corinthians 14:3 says, "But he who prophesies speaks edification and exhortation and comfort to men." A word from God should build up and encourage people. A comment may be from the flesh or an evil spirit if it is judgmental and condemning.

First John 4:1–3 says, "Beloved, do not believe every spirit, but test the spirits, whether they are of God; because many false prophets have gone out into the world. By this you will know the Spirit of God: Every spirit that confesses that Jesus Christ has come in the flesh is of God. And every spirit that does not confess that Jesus Christ has come in the flesh is not of God. And this is the spirit of the Antichrist, which you have heard was coming, and is now already in the world." Believers full of the Holy Spirit want to talk about Jesus. If a professed Christian shows little to no interest in glorifying or getting to know Jesus, that person may not be born–again.

Prayer Point: Father, help me to discern the Holy Spirit's voice and give me the grace to follow His leading.

CHAPTER 7 KEY POINTS
The Holy Spirit's Voice

- ❖ Prophesying is speaking from the inspiration of the Holy Spirit.
- ❖ When believers prophesy, the Holy Spirit forms the message.
- ❖ Prophecy is one voice of the Holy Spirit thru believers.
- ❖ The unsaved can also prophesy because the Holy Spirit is upon all flesh.
- ❖ Another outstanding way the Holy Spirit speaks through a person is when they speak in tongues.
- ❖ The Holy Spirit's voice also can be discerned by what He does.
- ❖ In the Scriptures, the Holy Spirit is: Teacher, Helper, Intercessor, Standby, Sanctifier, Advocate, Comforter, and Counselor.
- ❖ Someone speaking by the Holy Spirit may speak boldly and powerfully.
- ❖ When led by the Holy Spirit, a believer may do something out of the ordinary.
- ❖ The Holy Spirit may bring to remembrance something a person hasn't thought about in years.
- ❖ God wants to help people. He may use believers' life experiences to build up another person.
- ❖ If a believer's words do not glorify the Lord Jesus, the message may not be from the Holy Spirit.
- ❖ Believers can pray for the gift of discernment to help differentiate between a human spirit, the Holy Spirit, and an evil spirit
- ❖ A comment may be from the flesh or an evil spirit if it is judgmental and condemning.
- ❖ Believers full of the Holy Spirit want to talk about Jesus. If someone doesn't talk about Jesus, that person may not be born–again.

CHAPTER 7 STUDY QUESTIONS
The Holy Spirit's Voice

1. When a person speaks from inspiration of the Holy Spirit, they are _____.

2. Is prophecy a voice of the Holy Spirit? Yes No

3. Can someone Baptized in the Holy Spirit prophesy? Yes No

4. Can the unsaved prophesy? Yes No

5. Name 8 operations of the Holy Spirit

   _____
   _____
   _____

6. Who forms the language when a believer is speaking in tongues?

   _____
   _____
   _____

7. When led by the Holy Spirit, what might a believer expect?

   _____
   _____
   _____

8. If believers are full of the Holy Spirit, who will be glorified?

   _____

CHAPTER

Other Voices

There are, it may be, so many kinds of voices in the world, and none of them is without signification.
—1 Corinthians 14:10

The Voices of Allies.

Did you know that believers can have a belief that is not their own? Input from family, friends, and significant others can leave an enduring impact. The message may be positive (e.g., You have a bright future; Don't give up your dreams), neutral (e.g., Thank you for your attention to this matter), or negative (e.g., Your controlling nature is not helping us get along). Hurtful messages can go deep into the heart. Statements such as, you aren't good enough, you are ugly, there is something wrong with you, or you aren't smart enough leave wounds. Sometimes, the input from those closest to us leaves the most significant impact. The unconscious adoption of the voices, attitudes, emotions, perceptions, ideas, or traits of others is called "introjection." Children typically internalize parental morals, values, and beliefs without much processing.

The Voices of Adversaries.

Believers are also exposed to voices of adversaries. For example, I worked with a client once who overheard a conversation between his boss and another employee. His boss made derogatory comments about his work and even put down his personality. For weeks, my client said he was offended, depressed, bitter, and angry. He questioned whether or not he should continue in the company. He even thought about how he could avoid talking to his boss. The negative words spoken were like poison to his soul and hung over him like a dark cloud. He ended up leaving the company. His boss's words ruined their working relationship.

When Balak, king of Moab, hired Balaam to curse Israel, he hired Balaam as an adversarial voice. Numbers 22:6 says, "Therefore, please come at once, curse these people for me, for they are too mighty for me… for I know he whom you bless is blessed, and he whom you curse is cursed." Balak knew the power of words. He intended to harm Israel with spoken words. Consider Elisha. He was called bald by children. He "cursed" them and they were mauled by bears (2nd Kings 2:23-24).

Spoken words can turn into reality. Job 22:28 says, "You will also declare a thing, and it will be established for you; so light will shine on your ways." Spoken words have creative power. The creation account shows God speaking and things manifesting (Genesis 1:3). Jesus spoke to a fig tree, "Let no one eat fruit from you ever again"(Mark 11:14). When the disciples passed by the fig tree again, Peter exclaimed "Rabbi, look! The fig tree which You cursed has withered away"(Mark 11:21). Words can bring life or death (Proverbs 18:21: "Death and life are in the power of the tongue, and those who love it will eat its fruit"). Believers must be conscientious about what they say.

Spirit of the World.

First Corinthians 2:12 says, "Now we have received, not the spirit of the world, but the Spirit who is from God, that we might know the things that have been freely given to us by God." There is a spirit of the world. Think of what the world is about. It's not about God. It's about carnal things.

OTHER VOICES

The world has a way of working and communicating. Advertisements are everywhere and speak loudly: eat this, drink that, wear these, go there. So many directives. Some messages of the world get into the mind without people realizing it.

We live in a time of too many choices. Ephesians 2:1–2 says, "And you He made alive, who were dead in trespasses and sins, in which you once walked according to the course of this world, according to the prince of the power of the air, the spirit who now works in the sons of disobedience." The course of this world is what is happening outside of the church. Most of it is consumerism and a "Me, Me, Me" mentality. First John 2:16 says, "For all that is in the world—the lust of the flesh, the lust of the eyes, and the pride of life—is not of the Father but is of the world."

The lust of the eyes is the desire to possess. When a person goes to a store or restaurant, the lust of the eyes may speak (e.g., how pretty, that looks good, I need that). Lust of the eyes is difficult to manage. People's eyes are open about 16 hours a day. Being able to say "no" is one of the best defenses against lust of the eyes.

Pride of life also has a voice. Pride of life is of the world and leads people to believe they are great because of their achievements. Pride of life can be subtle, but basically says, look at me and take notice of what I have done. Nebuchadnezzar suffered from pride of life and had thoughts stemming from that condition. Daniel 4:30 says, "The king spoke, saying, 'Is not this great Babylon, that I have built for a royal dwelling by my mighty power and for the honor of my majesty?'" This ruler was bragging about what he had done. Haman also suffered from pride of life. Esther 5:10–12 says,

> Nevertheless Haman restrained himself and went home, and he sent and called for his friends and his wife Zeresh. Then Haman told them of his great riches, the multitude of his children, everything in which the king had promoted him, and how he had advanced him above the officials and servants of the king. Moreover Haman said, Besides, Queen Esther invited no one but me to come in with the

king to the banquet that she prepared; and tomorrow I am again invited by her, along with the king.

Haman was puffed up and full of himself. He gushed about all the things pointing to his supposed greatness. Spiritually, he was on a dangerous precipice. Proverbs 16:18-19 says, "Pride goes before destruction, and a haughty spirit before a fall. It is surely "better to be of a humble spirit with the lowly, than to divide the spoil with the proud" (Proverbs 16:19).

King Hezekiah may have suffered pride of life. Consider what he did with the Babylonian envoys. 2nd Kings 20:13 says, "And Hezekiah was attentive to them, and showed them all the house of his treasures – the silver and gold, the spices and precious ointment, and all his armory – all that was found among his treasures. There was nothing in his house or in all his dominion that Hezekiah did not show them." Hezekiah showed them everything. Can you imagine letting strangers in your house and showing them what was in every room? Prophet Isaiah came and asked Hezekiah what he had shown his guests. He also told Hezekiah that all would be taken, including some of his descendants. Second Kings 20:16–18 says, "Then Isaiah said to Hezekiah, 'Hear the word of the Lord: Behold the days are coming when all that is in your house, and what your fathers have accumulated until this day, shall be carried to Babylon; nothing shall be left,' says the Lord. 'And they shall take away some of your sons who will descend from you, whom you will beget; and they shall be eunuchs in the palace of the king of Babylon.'" In this case, there was a significant consequence for pride of life. Hezekiah eventually lost everything.

Evil Spirits.

Evil spirits have a voice and can speak to the minds of believers. Ananias heard from a spirit. Peter says it was "Satan." Acts 5:1–4 says,

> But a certain man named Ananias, with Sapphira his wife, sold a possession. And he kept back part of the proceeds, his wife also being aware of it, and brought a certain part and laid it at the apostles' feet. But Peter said, Ananias,

why has Satan filled your heart to lie to the Holy Spirit and keep back part of the price of the land for yourself? While it remained, was it not your own? And after it was sold, was it not in your own control? Why have you conceived this thing in your heart? You have not lied to men but to God.

Evil spirits can also speak through believers. Luke 4:33–34 says, "Now in the synagogue there was a man who had a spirit of an unclean demon. And he cried out with a loud voice, saying, 'Let us alone! What have we to do with You, Jesus of Nazareth? Did You come to destroy us? I know who You are—the Holy One of God!'" This passage shows a spirit speaking out of someone. Luke 4:35–36 says, "But Jesus rebuked him, saying, 'Be quiet, and come out of him!' And when the demon had thrown him in their midst, it came out of him and did not hurt him. Then they were all amazed and spoke among themselves, saying, 'What a word this is! For with authority and power He commands the unclean spirits, and they come out.'" The man of the Gadarenes had a demon speaking through him. Mark 5:6–7 says, "When he saw Jesus from afar, he ran and worshiped Him. And he cried out with a loud voice and said, 'What have I to do with You, Jesus, Son of the Most High God? I implore You by God that You do not torment me.'" The man ran to Jesus for help. The demons were in terror wanting Jesus to leave.

Ministry-wise, believers must be careful who they follow. Not every minister is God–approved. First John 4:1 says, "Beloved do not believe every spirit, but test the spirits, whether they are of God; because many false prophets have gone out into the world." This verse shows that some people will not be true prophets. What they share may not reflect God's word or heart.

Prayer Point: Father, reveal to me any voices that may be competing with Your truth and direction for my life.

CHAPTER 8 KEY POINTS
Other Voices

- Input from family, friends, and significant others can leave an enduring impact.
- Hurtful messages can go deep into the heart.
- Sometimes, the input from those closest to us leaves the most significant impact.
- The unconscious adoption of the voices, attitudes, emotions, perceptions, ideas, or traits of others is called "Introjection."
- Spoken words have creative power.
- Job 22:28 says, "You will also declare a thing, and it will be established for you; so light will shine on your ways."
- Some messages of the world get into the mind without people realizing it.
- The lust of the eyes is the desire to possess.
- Pride of life is of the world and leads people to believe they are great because of their achievements.
- Evil spirits have a voice and can speak to the minds of believers.
- Evil spirits can also speak through believers.
- Believers must be careful who they follow. Not every minister is God–approved.

CHAPTER 8 STUDY QUESTIONS
Other Voices

1. List three sources of worldly beliefs.

2. Define introjection.

3. Can words have creative power? Yes No

4. Write one verse from the book of Genesis that shows the power of words.

5. What is the spirit of the world?

6. How can a believer resist the lust of the eyes?

   _____
   _____
   _____
   _____

7. Name three people in the Bible who suffered pride of life.

   _____
   _____
   _____
   _____

8. Write one Bible verse that depicts an evil spirit affecting someone's thinking.

   _____
   _____
   _____
   _____

PART 3

Heart Conditions

CHAPTER 9

Heart Wounds

He heals the brokenhearted and binds up their wounds.
—Psalm 147:3

Like a vital organ, the soul has much to do in reacting and dealing with life's challenges daily. It takes in, processes, and makes sense out of many pieces of input. A healthy soul quickly deals with external and internal stresses and pressures. Thoughts flow easily. Emotions are present and normative. In contrast, a wounded soul tends to struggle and sometimes fails in dealing with day-to-day events. Thoughts may race. Confusion may set in. Emotions can be all over the place or not present at all.

The mind, emotions, or will can be wounded. When the mind is wounded, people may have trouble managing their thoughts, suffer negative beliefs, experience attention and memory problems, and feel like they are in their heads often. When the emotions are wounded, people may experience extreme emotions, widely fluctuating emotions that don't fit a situation, lack of emotions, or painful emotions. When the will is wounded, people can have trouble directing their behavior; they may do things but don't know why, feel more willful, and be guided mainly by their emotions.

Heart wounds happen when a life event (personal or impersonal) injures the soul. For example, being in a terrible car accident could make it hard for someone to ride in a car. Rather than having peaceful thoughts, that person might suffer dread-filled thoughts about riding in a car. Emotionally, the person previously in a car accident may have intense fear when getting in a car rather than calm. That person may also exercise their will differently (e.g., decline car rides) to avoid being in another accident. When peoples' thoughts, emotions, or will are significantly affected by a life event, sometimes it is an indicator that the soul is wounded.

Heart wounds are often caused by situations that overwhelm the soul. A person may trip and fall into a pile of leaves while walking through a wooded area. A fall may cause some physical pain, but it will probably not injure the soul. However, if a person trips and falls running from a bear, breaks an ankle, needs surgery and physical therapy, and then loses their job, this person may have a heart wound. They may be unable to go in wooded areas for fear of an animal attack. The person may have physical and psychological signs of anxiety being outdoors. That person may develop extreme or unreasonable beliefs (e.g., "If I go for a walk, I will be attacked").

Heart wounds can be identified by the symptoms they cause. For most people, talking about walking in the woods probably wouldn't elicit any significant reaction. However, the person who fell while running from a bear may start to shake and tremble. That person may change the topic or even leave the room. These symptoms would be a sign that there is a wound in the heart.

Soul wounds can also come from within when the mind creates overwhelming thoughts and beliefs. For example, a person may have a mole on their arm and believe it is cancer. Repetitive thoughts about dying from cancer would wound the soul. Can you imagine the constant terror and dread? It would probably be hard for that person to have positive feelings. While working in a psychiatric unit, I met a man who thought he ran over someone whenever he drove his car. This troubling thought was taking away all his peace. His soul was wounded from within.

Soul Splits.

Did you know that a person's soul wound could be a split? Dissociative disorders are a severe mental illness in which people lose connection between thoughts, emotions, behavior, and identity. When I was a psychology intern, I met an adult woman previously diagnosed with multiple personality disorder (now known as dissociative identity disorder) in a psychiatric unit. I was asked to assess how she was doing. I entered her room to find her barricaded behind a wall of pillows. She seemed to be in a part of her personality that was full of fear. After a few minutes, she peaked her head up, and a tear rolled down her cheek. She spoke in a shaky, little child's voice briefly and then tucked herself away again. A few minutes later, she spoke again, but the voice was different. More commanding. Less distant. She made intense eye contact. This seemed like a protective personality. From what I experienced in my time with her, the dissociative identity disorder diagnosis did seem to fit. She had a severe case of a soul split.

As a psychologist, I've identified milder cases of soul-splitting. For example, I met a man whose father had severely beaten him throughout his childhood. This man didn't seem to have different personalities. But his soul seemed split in various ways. His beliefs were sharply divided. All men were viewed as mean and violent. He didn't have any positive thoughts about male friends or colleagues. His emotions seemed split. Positive emotions were nonexistent. He mainly had anxiety and fear. Anger was notably absent. Behaviorally, he appeared ready to avoid or attack, which contrasted with his generally easy-going and gregarious personality.

I met a middle-aged woman who men had repeatedly hurt. Her father made her the peacemaker in his marriage to her mother. He insisted she take his side; if she didn't, he would be cold, distant, and punitive. As an adult, her boyfriends lied to her and cheated on her. She had yet to have a successful relationship. Her soul was deeply wounded. Her behavior, at times, did not line up with her beliefs. She wanted to be friendly towards her current boyfriend but was irritable, testy, jealous, and suspicious. Emotionally, she was up and down. She was rageful towards her father and passive-aggressive, suspicious, and untrusting of her current boyfriend. She didn't have dissociative identity disorder, but her soul had sharply divided parts.

With Christian clients, I at times I sense a soul split of fear versus faith in certain areas. When clients are in the fear part of their soul, their mindsets, thoughts, and imaginations are often provoking fear which is a strong emotion associated with a perceived threat of danger or pain. When clients are in the faith based part of their soul, their mindsets thoughts and imaginations are provoking a sense of confidence in God. When someone has a fear/faith split, what that person says one day may not match what they say on another day. It takes time to build faith for something, so this kind of split is not necessarily a bad thing. It certainly could point to a problem if fear was outweighing faith.

Spirit–Soul Split.

In a spirit–soul split, people may feel one way in their spirit about something but feel differently in their soul. For example, believers may have peace about following God's leading to attend a prayer group, but in their soul, they may feel a lack of desire to go to the prayer group. They may even experience frustration or feelings of alienation during the prayer group. With a spirit–soul split, people can experience intense inner distress. Jonah comes to mind. God gave him a command, but he ran the other way. Jonah 1:2-3 says, "'Arise, go to Nineveh, that great city, and cry out against it; for their wickedness has come up before Me.' But Jonah arose to flee to Tarshish from the presence of the LORD…" It seemed like his spirit was attuned to God, but his soul did not want to obey. All believers might suffer a spirit-soul split from time to time. Matthew 26:41 says, "Watch and pray, lest you enter into temptation. The spirit indeed is willing, but the flesh is weak." The spirit will want to obey God, but the soul and body may not.

Soul Wound Impact.

The impact of soul wounds on people's lives vary widely. Some life events change the whole course of life. Becoming a quadraplegic after a car accident would undoubtedly reflect a considerable impact. I met a lovely lady raised by a father with schizophrenia. Her father was often paranoid, rigid, confused, and overly emotional. She was glad to get through childhood. In general, she did well in her social life. However, in certain interpersonal situations, this lady would psychologically deteriorate. She would rage, shut down, or be unable to think clearly. She likely had one or more soul wounds from being raised by a father with a severe mental illness.

Wounds from various traumatic life events (e.g., child abuse, betrayal, war, natural disasters) can remain in the soul for many years. I met someone who was tearful very soon into our conversation. He quickly blurted out that he had found his son dead while on a camping trip. I was shocked. He talked about how difficult it had been to find his son near their campfire. His sobbing and shaking made me think that his son died recently. When I finally asked when his son had passed, the man said, "About 20 years ago." That was not the answer I expected. His soul was wounded and never got better. The man said he had never talked about what happened with anyone. The event was completely unprocessed and was causing inner turmoil and unrest.

I met a young woman who said she became unusually depressed and angry when she saw a cat carrying a chipmunk in his mouth outside her window. We talked about the matter, and, as a child, this woman recalled watching chipmunks play outside her window. Her parents were together at that time, and she remembered feeling happy. However, when her parents separated, this girl said she was forced to move. She remembers crying for days when told she had to relocate. For her, the chipmunks represented family, peace, happiness, and home. All that was taken away. Seeing a cat carrying away a chipmunk brought up painful feelings associated with having to abruptly move away from her beloved home. She still had a soul wound.

Remember the old idiom, "Charging a 500–dollar fine for a 10–cent crime." A disproportionate reaction to a situation can suggest a heart wound. I remember a case of a woman who said she had a massive argument with her husband that lasted for days. I asked her what happened, and she said he wanted to watch a TV show. I asked her what transpired during the show, and she said one of the women in the show was named Barbara. Still not getting it, I asked what upset her, and she said she couldn't believe he wanted to watch a show with a woman named Barbara. She elaborated and revealed that three years ago, she found her husband exchanging loving texts with a woman named Barbara. This woman was still irate and offended about what he had done. His emotional adultery deeply wounded her soul.

I've met people with heart wounds from love hunger. Severely neglected by her sick and selfish husband, I knew one woman who went on to behave in ways she felt awful about. She had developed an emotional affair with someone at her gym, and was also texting an old high school flame. Her feelings of guilt and shame were overwhelming at times. I met a man who found out his wife had been talking to another man right after they got home from their honeymoon. Devastated, this man went on to harbor such anger and bitterness, that he didn't even want to be around his wife. He found every excuse to not be home, and when he was home he was always working. There were no loving exchanges, words, or affection. He developed an eating disorder as well as a problem with alcohol. This hurt his self esteem and sense of goodness. Thus, the heart can be wounded from a lack of love and the subsequent compensatory behaviors.

Soul Wound Management.

Soul wounds can be difficult to manage. Sometimes, people don't even realize they have wounds. Some heart wounds never get better despite attempts at talk therapy, stress management, exercise, or other self help strategies. People may give up hope that their hearts can be healed. But God. Psalm 147:3 says, "He [God] heals the brokenhearted and binds up their wounds." "Binds up" in this verse is "chabash," which means "to bandage, wrap, and bring relief." The word "wounds" in this verse is "atstsebeth" which means "hurts, injuries, and pains." God is all about bringing help and treatment to the injuries and pains of believers' souls.

Did you ever get a deep cut on your skin? The steps to cleaning the wound were not pain free ones. You had to wash the wound with soap and water, dry it off, put on antibiotic, and then a bandage to protect it. Then you had to wash the wound and change the dressing regularly until the wound was no longer open. Some physical wounds heal within days, others take longer.

Some wounds actually get worse over time. They become red, swollen, painful, and infected. Some wounds need professional care to ensure full healing. Big wounds usually always need professional care from the start to promote healing.

Like physical wounds, soul wounds need meticulous care. Soul wounds must be rinsed too, which is done by talking. People can release pent-up emotions and organize their thoughts by sharing about painful events. They can develop a healthy narrative about what happened and release mindsets and attitudes that may be unhealthy. The soap for a soul wound would be deep processing. It's getting into the nitty gritty of an overwhelming or traumatic situation and its impact on someone's psychology. Consider how upset a person may be after an assault and car theft—so much pain and suffering. The person may have negative emotions, nightmares, and flashbacks. The person may initially feel glad to be alive. But over time, the person may notice increasing psychological problems, including offense, anger, pride, and angst about the justice system. This person's soul would likely benefit from talking through the assault and subsequent experiences. Bringing the matter to God in prayer would also be an essential step in the heart wound recovery process.

Prayer Point: Father, reveal to me the wounds in my heart and show me Your path of healing.

CHAPTER 9 KEY POINTS
Heart Wounds

- A wounded soul tends to struggle and sometimes fails in dealing with day-to-day events.
- The mind, emotions, or will can be wounded.
- Heart wounds happen when a life event (personal or impersonal) injures the soul.
- Heart wounds can be identified by the symptoms they cause.
- Soul wounds can also come from within when the mind creates overwhelming thoughts and beliefs.
- A person's soul wound could be a split.
- When someone has a fear/faith split, what that person says one day may not match what they say on another day.
- In a spirit-soul split, people may feel one way in their spirit about something but feel differently in their soul.
- The spirit will want to obey God, but the soul and body may not.
- The impact of soul wounds on people's lives vary widely.
- A disproportionate reaction to a situation can suggest a heart wound.
- The heart can be wounded from a lack of love and the subsequent compensatory behaviors.
- Some heart wounds never get better despite attempts at talk therapy, stress management, exercise, or other self help strategies.
- God is all about bringing help and treatment to the injuries and pains of believers' souls.
- Like physical wounds, soul wounds need meticulous care.

CHAPTER 9 STUDY QUESTIONS
Heart Wounds

1. Define a heart wound.

   _____
   _____
   _____
   _____

2. Can overwhelming situations wound the soul? Yes No

3. How can believers identify a heart wound?

   _____
   _____
   _____
   _____

4. Do heart wounds get better on their own? Yes No

5. Could a disproportionate reaction to a situation suggest a heart wound? Yes No

6. Write out Psalm 147:3.

   _____
   _____
   _____
   _____

7. Describe what God can do to help heal heart wounds.

_____
_____
_____
_____

CHAPTER

Heartcry

*Deep calls unto deep at the noise of Your waterfalls;
all Your waves and billows have gone over me.*
—Psalm 42:7

Have you ever been in a dire situation? Do you remember what happened deep inside? While responses vary, a desperate plea can arise. It can feel powerful and from a person's core. This inward cry is a "heartcry." A heartcry is distinct. If someone isn't familiar with how the soul and body work, it can be mistaken for a thought, feeling, or physical urge. Heartcry comes from a person's spirit. Psalm 130:1–2 says, "Out of the depths I have cried to You, O LORD; Lord, hear my voice! Let Your ears be attentive to the voice of my supplications." Out of what depths? The depths of the heart. The spirit. The inner man. Psalm 42:7 says, "Deep calls unto deep…" That's a picture of heartcry. Deep (the human spirit) calling to deep (Holy Spirit).

Heartcry is not an intellectual matter. It's not a "headcry." Heartcry doesn't come from the brain. Heartcry is from the innermost being. A believer may ponder something, and it may not affect the spirit. Remember the phrase, "All head, no heart?" That's when a person is thinking just intellectually. That is not heartcry. A heartcry can become a prayer when a person directs it toward God.

The Bible is full of examples of heartcries. I think of David when I think of heartcry. He was a worshiper of God. He played music and danced before the Lord. David was after God's heart. He knew about deep calling unto deep. Acts 13:22 says, "And when He had removed him [Saul], He raised up for them David as king, to whom He also gave testimony and said, 'I have found David the son of Jesse, a man after My own heart who will do all my will.'"

David received anointing to be the next king. For years, he was running from a murderous king who did not want to be displaced. Most people have not experienced that level of torment and oppression. He was being hunted down and often in hiding. Imagine the angst, fear, and terror David must have felt. King David's life situation led to many heart cries. Psalm 61:1–2 says, "Hear my cry, O God; Attend to my prayer. From the end of the earth I will cry to You, when my heart is overwhelmed; lead me to the rock that is higher than I." Psalm 12:1 says, "Help, LORD, for the godly man ceases! For the faithful disappear from among the sons of men." Psalm 13:1 says, "How long, O LORD? Will You forget me forever? How long will You hide your face from me? Psalm 18:3 says, "I will call upon the Lord who is worthy to be praised; So shall I be saved from my enemies." David likely called upon the Lord from his spirit.

Overwhelming life situations can set up conditions for heartcry. Consider someone who develops a throat cancer. For months, the person may struggle to eat a piece of fruit or bowl of soup. The weight loss is dramatic, and anorexia has set in. The person's soul may have many painful thoughts (e.g., "Why is this happening to me? When will this end? I can't take this anymore"). The emotions may include fear, confusion, and grief. Under such duress, a person's spirit may cry to God for healing and comfort. Imagine a person discovering their spouse is cheating. Shock, confusion, and painful feelings erupt. The person may cry, "God, I am crushed. Help me get through this devastating situation." Psalm 121:1–2 says, "I will lift up my eyes to the hills – from whence comes my help? My help comes from the LORD, who made heaven and earth."

Consider the heartcry of Hagar. She wasn't an Israelite and had no status or covenant relationship with God. She was watching her baby die and cried out in anguish. God heard her child's cry. Hagar gives God a name – "the God who sees me." Genesis 21:14–16 says,

> So Abraham rose early in the morning, and took bread and a skin of water; and putting it on her shoulder, he gave it and the boy to Hagar, and sent her away. Then she departed and wandered in the Wilderness of Beersheba. And the water in the skin was used up, and she placed the boy under one of the shrubs. Then she went and sat down across from him at a distance of about a bowshot; for she said to herself, "Let me not see the death of the boy." So she sat opposite him, and lifted her voice and wept. And God heard the voice of the lad. Then the angel of God called to Hagar out of heaven, and said to her, "What ails you, Hagar? Fear not, for God has heard the voice of the lad where he is. Arise, lift up the lad and hold him with your hand, for I will make him a great nation.

Heartcry often arises when people come to the end of themselves. People with unrelenting problems become desperate. Heartcry says, "I can't deal with this Lord, but I know you can. Please help me!" Consider the heartcry of Hannah. She was barren and had to watch another woman repeatedly bear children. First Samuel 1:11–13 says,

> Then she made a vow and said, O LORD of hosts, if You will indeed look on the affliction of Your maidservant and remember me and not forget Your maidservant, but will give Your maidservant a male child, then I will give him to the LORD all the days of his life, and no razor shall come upon his head. And it happened, as she continued praying before the LORD, that Eli watched her mouth. Now Hannah spoke in her heart; only her lips moved, but her voice was not heard. Therefore Eli thought she was drunk.

In the depths of her being, Hannah cried out to the Lord. We know God heard her because she conceived. First Samuel 1:19–20 says, "Then they rose early in the morning and worshiped before the LORD and returned and came to their house at Ramah. And Elkanah knew Hannah his wife, and the LORD remembered her. So it came to pass in the process of time that Hannah conceived and bore a son, and called his name Samuel, saying, Because I have asked for him from the LORD."

Prayer Point: Father, show me the cries in my heart and teach me how to direct these cries to You.

CHAPTER 10 KEY POINTS
Heartcry

- A heartcry comes from a person's spirit.
- Psalm 42:7 says, "deep calls unto deep…" That's a picture of heartcry. Deep (the human spirit) calling to deep (Holy Spirit).
- Heartcry is not an intellectual matter. It's not coming from the brain.
- Heartcry comes from the innermost being.
- A heartcry can become a prayer when a person directs it towards God.
- The Bible is full of examples of heartcries.
- King David's life situation led to many heart cries.
- Overwhelming life situations can set up conditions for heartcry.
- Consider the heartcry of Hagar. She wasn't an Israelite and had no status or covenant relationship with God. She was watching her baby die and cried out in anguish.
- Heartcry often arises when people come to the end of themselves.
- A heartcry basically says, "I can't deal with this, but LORD I know you can. Please help me!"
- Consider the heartcry of Hannah. She was barren and had to watch another woman repeatedly bear children.
- Hannah spoke in her heart. In the very depth of her being she cried out to the Lord.

CHAPTER 10 STUDY QUESTIONS
Heartcry

1. Define heartcry.

2. Where does a heartcry emanate from?

3. Write out two Bible verses that demonstrate heartcry.

4. Is heartcry a prayer? Yes No

5. Is heartcry a headcry? Yes No

6. Name and describe two women in the Bible who cried out to God for help.

_____
_____
_____
_____

7. Can heartcries arise when believers come to the end of themselves? Yes No

CHAPTER

Heart Sickness

*Hope deferred makes the heart sick, but when
the desire comes, it is a tree of life.*
—Proverbs 13:12

Did you know that your heart can get sick? It absolutely can. The problem with heart sickness is that it can go on for weeks, months, or even years. Certain conditions make it more likely that the heart will get sick. One situation is when people want something, but they never get it. For example, a person may be hoping for a loving and secure family life, a beautiful marriage, the salvation of a family member, a great job, financial freedom, or a baby. The person waits and waits, and nothing arrives. Ouch. When believers' hopes are not fulfilled, it can make the heart sick.

Proverbs 13:12 says, "Hope deferred makes the heart sick, but when the desire comes, it is a tree of life." When things get delayed, drawn out, or prolonged, the heart takes a hit. When someone has heart sickness, that person can feel weak and unwell. That person may not have vibrancy and zest for life. Someone with heart sickness can function but may feel sluggish and dull.

Consider Abraham. He may have suffered from heart sickness. Genesis 15:1–3 says, "After these things the word of the LORD came to Abram in a vision, saying, 'Do not be afraid, Abram. I am your shield, your exceedingly great reward.' But Abram said, 'Lord GOD, what will You give me, seeing I go childless, and the heir of my house is Eliezer of Damascus?' Then Abram said, 'Look, You have given me no offspring; indeed one born in my house is my heir!'" God speaks promises of protection and provision to Abram. Likely due to heart sickness, Abram essentially ignores what God says and focuses on his lack of children. Abraham was 75 when he first received the promise of a child and was 100 when Isaac was born. Such a long delay likely made his heart sick.

I've met believers who had heart sickness. After months or years of waiting for physical or mental healing, financial blessings, and breakthrough, these people were sad, confused, and even annoyed. While no one wanted to let go of the promise made to them, I noticed that some had stopped believing. Heart sickness can put a damper on faith.

Another condition that can make the heart sick is sin. Consider the tribe of Judah. The people were in rebellion and waywardness. Their situations were dire. Isaiah 1:5–6 says, "Why should you be stricken again? You will revolt more and more. The whole head is sick, and the whole heart faints. From the sole of the foot even to the head, there is no soundness in it, but wounds and bruises and putrefying sores; they have not been closed or bound up, or soothed with ointment." Due to their sinful ways, the people of Judah were reaping rotten fruit and were suffering. The people were sin–sick. Their hearts were ill ("the whole head is sick and the whole heart faints").

When the heart is sick, people can develop mindsets that are unhealthy. The devil can also insert lies and evil thoughts into believers' minds during times of waiting. Being upset about unfulfilled promises can lead to thoughts such as, "life isn't worth living," or "my life doesn't matter." A negative mindset can become a stronghold. A stronghold is a territory in the mind that the devil controls. Thoughts coming from a stronghold usually don't align with God's Word. Strongholds are a big problem for believers because what a person thinks will determine what they believe, say, and do. (Luke 6:45 "...Out of the abundance of the heart his mouth speaks"; Proverbs 23:7 "For as he thinks in his heart, so is he...").

Strongholds won't go away on their own. Believers must destroy them with spiritual weapons. God teaches how to handle strongholds in 2nd Corinthians 10:4–5 ("For the weapons of our warfare are not carnal but mighty in God for pulling down strongholds, casting down arguments and every high thing that exalts itself against the knowledge of God, bringing every thought into captivity to the obedience of Christ"). Believers must pull down strongholds with the Word of God. The Word is the truth that sets believers free from wrong mindsets and lies. Faith (believing we have what we are hoping for before it comes), praise, worship, and the name of Jesus are also effective weapons.

For example, a believer could battle a stronghold belief that life isn't worth living by confessing the following Bible verses. A believer would say, "I want to live long on the earth because":

- Jeremiah 29:11 says, "For I know the thoughts that I think toward you, says the Lord, thoughts of peace and not of evil, to give you a future and a hope."
- Isaiah 46:3–4 says, "Listen to Me, O house of Jacob, and all the remnant of the house of Israel, who have been upheld by Me from birth, who have been carried from the womb: Even to your old age, I am He, and even to gray hairs I will carry you! I have made, and I will bear; even I will carry, and will deliver you."
- John 10:10 says, "The thief does not come except to steal, and to kill, and to destroy. I have come that they may have life, and that they may have it more abundantly."
- Isaiah 41:10 says, "Fear not, for I am with you; Be not dismayed, for I am your God. I will strengthen you, Yes, I will help you, I will uphold you with My righteous right hand."
- Psalm 55:22 says, "Cast your burden on the LORD, and He shall sustain you; He shall never permit the righteous to be moved."
- First John 4:4 says, "...He who is in you is greater than he that is in the world."
- Psalm 34:19 says, "Many are the afflictions of the righteous, but the LORD delivers him out of them all."
- Hebrews 13:5 says, "...I will never leave you nor forsake you."

Believers benefit from cultivating and maintaining faith that what they are hoping for will come. Believers must believe that God can deliver on His promises and they will have the desire of their hearts. If people continue to focus on what they don't have, they will feel empty and upset. If believers walk by faith and not sight, they can walk with fullness and joy.

Believers must be diligent to avoid a "hope deferred" mindset. It's all about perspective. Believers should focus on the truth of God's promises and not the natural reality, which is changeable. God never changes. He has obligated Himself to perform His Word (Hebrews 6:17). Does this mean God will fulfill every desire? No. That's why it is good to draw near to God to discover His will.

For example, say a young believer wants to be an evangelist. He wants to win souls for God on a massive scale. He imagines crusades and preaching in stadiums. He asks God to make him into an evangelist. He calls those things that are not as though they were. He waits a long time and wonders why nothing ever manifests. While everyone is to evangelize, only some are called to be evangelists. Believers need to find out who they are in Christ. Believing for something that isn't God's plan can cause heart sickness due to hope deferred.

Philippians 4:12–13 says, "I know how to be abased, and I know how to abound. Everywhere and in all things I have learned both to be full and to be hungry, both to abound and to suffer need. I can do all things through Christ who strengthens me." Being content is a heart attitude that can minimize heart sickness. It keeps believers mindful of what they have rather than what they don't.

The "I can do all things through Christ" verse requires cautious interpretation. This verse does not mean believers can do all things. Would someone who can't add well be a good accountant? No. Would a person who hates to read be a good book editor? No. What believers can do is adjust to conditions. They can adapt to riches and endure lean times. With God on our side, believers can face life as it comes.

Prayer Point: Father, please make my sick heart well again so I can praise You and find comfort in Your Promises.

CHAPTER 11 KEY POINTS
Heart Sickness

- ❖ When someone's hope is not fulfilled, it can make the heart sick.
- ❖ When things get delayed, drawn out, or prolonged the heart can become ill.
- ❖ Someone with heart sickness can function, but may feel sluggish and dull.
- ❖ Abraham was age 75 when he first received the promise of a child, and was 100 when Isaac was born. Such a long delay likely made his heart sick.
- ❖ Heart sickness can put a damper on faith.
- ❖ When the heart is sick, people can develop mindsets that are unhealthy.
- ❖ The devil can also insert lies and evil thoughts into believers' minds during times of waiting.
- ❖ Strongholds won't go away on their own.
- ❖ Believers must pull down strongholds with the Word of God.
- ❖ The Word is the truth that sets believers free from wrong mind sets and Satan's lies.
- ❖ Believers benefit from cultivating and maintaining faith that what they are hoping for will come.
- ❖ Believers should focus on the truth of God's promises and not the natural reality, which is changeable.

CHAPTER 11 STUDY QUESTIONS
Heart Sickness

1. Define heart sickness.

2. What are two potential causes of heart sickness?

3. What may have caused Abraham's heart to get sick?

4. Can heart sickness affect faith? Yes No

5. Can a believer with heart sickness have negative mindsets? Yes No

6. Describe how a believer can address problematic thoughts associated with heart sickness.

_____
_____
_____
_____

7. How can a believer minimize a "hope deferred" mindset?

_____
_____
_____
_____

8. Being _____ is a heart attitude that can minimize heart sickness.

CHAPTER 12

Heart Failure

Hear my cry, O God; attend to my prayer. From the end of the earth I will cry to You, when my heart is overwhelmed; Lead me to the rock that is higher than I.
—Psalm 61:1–2

When someone has physical heart failure, their heart is no longer contracting well enough to get sufficient oxygen and blood to the organs. The heart is still beating but not at capacity. When heart failure happens, other parts of the body are affected. It's like a car engine that hasn't had an oil change in a while. It starts and runs, but not efficiently.

Heart failure can happen to the soul. When believers have heart failure, their ability to manage their mind, emotions, and will breaks down. When the soul fails, feelings of overwhelming fatigue and reduced ability to manage stress and exertion are present. Psalm 61 shows someone who may have been suffering heart failure. Verses 1–2 (New International Version) says, "Hear my cry, O God; listen to my prayer. From the ends of the earth I call to you. I call as my heart grows faint; lead me to the rock that is higher than I." Most people have become physically faint at some point. The world grew dim while consciousness faded. In these situations, people need physical support or someone to bring them to a chair. When the soul feels like it can't go on, it also needs reliable support and encouragement.

Another image of heart failure could be Psalm 22. Some scholars interpret this passage to be a Messianic psalm foretelling Jesus's crucifixion. Psalm 22:14 says, "I am poured out like water, and all My bones are out of joint. My heart has turned to wax; it has melted within Me." A heart like wax is a heart that has become numb. It is so overwhelmed it doesn't feel much. A heart that has "melted" suggests things have gotten out of order. The soul is still working, but not very well. A numb heart makes me think of someone dissociating under extreme stress.

Elijah may have suffered heart failure. First Kings 19:4 says, "But he himself went a day's journey into the wilderness, and came and sat down under a broom tree. And he prayed that he might die, and said, "It is enough! Now, LORD, take my life, for I am no better than my fathers!" Elijah just had a showdown with the prophets of Baal at Carmel. Jezebel threatened to take his life. Elijah's heart became overwhelmed and started to fail. His heart was so distraught that he thought about dying. He even asked God to end his life. Now, that is someone whose heart is shutting down.

Moses also faced overwhelming circumstances. Numbers 11:11–15 says,

> So Moses said to the LORD, "Why have You afflicted Your servant? And why have I not found favor in Your sight, that You have laid the burden of all these people on me? Did I conceive all these people? Did I beget them, that You should say to me, 'Carry them in your bosom, as a guardian carries a nursing child,' to the land which You swore to their fathers? Where am I to get meat to give to all these people? For they weep all over me, saying, 'Give us meat, that we may eat.' I am not able to bear all these people alone, because the burden is too heavy for me. If You treat me like this, please kill me here and now —if I have found favor in Your sight—and do not let me see my wretchedness!"

Moses' soul started to fail because of the massive burden of leading the Israelites. It is hard to deal with a few people. Imagine directing about 600,000. And not virtually or through a park. Moses guided a nation through unknown territory. Deserts. Wilderness. Plus, Moses just led Israel through devastating plagues in Egypt. He was dealing with a large group of stressed people, probably full of fear and angst.

Consider Jonah. He ran from God and ended up in the belly of a whale. It seems absurd that God called Jonah to go one way, and he went another. He didn't want to preach to Nineveh. Jonah 2:7 says, "When my soul fainted within me, I remembered the Lord; And my prayer went up to You, into Your holy temple." Jonah's situation overwhelmed him, and he said his "soul fainted." His heart was failing. He probably was losing hope. Fortunately, he called on God and was rescued him from his horrendous situation. God is so good, especially to those who call on Him in their time of dire need.

Prayer Point: Father, revive my failing heart so that I can run the race You have set before me.

CHAPTER 12 KEY POINTS
Heart Failure

- ❖ Heart failure can happen to the soul.
- ❖ When believers have heart failure, their ability to manage the mind, emotions, and will starts to break down.
- ❖ When the soul fails, feelings of overwhelming fatigue and reduced ability to manage stress and exertion are present.
- ❖ When the soul feels like it can't go on, it needs reliable support and encouragement.
- ❖ Psalm 22:14 says, "I am poured out like water, and all My bones are out of joint; My heart is like wax; it has melted within Me."
- ❖ A heart like wax is a heart that has become numb. It is so overwhelmed it doesn't feel much.
- ❖ A numb heart makes me think of someone dissociating under extreme stress.
- ❖ Elijah's heart was overwhelmed and started to fail.
- ❖ Moses is another example of someone who may have suffered heart failure.
- ❖ Moses' soul started to fail because of the great burden of leading the Israelites.
- ❖ Jonah's situation overwhelmed him and he said his "soul fainted."

CHAPTER 12 STUDY QUESTIONS
Heart Failure

1. What happens when heart failure affects the soul?

2. Describe two symptoms of heart failure in the soul.

3. Write out Psalm 61:1–2 (NIV) and Psalm 22:14 (these are images of heart failure).

HEART FAILURE

4. What life situation of Elijah contributed to symptoms of heart failure?
   _____
   _____
   _____
   _____

5. Did Elijah and Moses get so overwhelmed that they wanted to die? Yes No

6. Why did Jonah's soul faint within him?
   _____
   _____
   _____
   _____

13
CHAPTER

Heartbreak

A merry heart makes a cheerful countenance,
but by sorrow of the heart the spirit is broken.
—Proverbs 15:13

When life circumstances crush believers' souls, and they cannot function, they are now experiencing heartbreak. This condition is worse than heart failure because a person can still manage to do things with heart failure. In heartbreak, believers often can't even do the basics. Sudden traumatic life events such as the death of a loved one in an accident, a divorce summons, being fired from a job for no apparent reason, or a devastating house fire can cause heartbreak. The unexpected loss of valuable relationships and possessions crushes the mind and emotions. Believers may not be able to eat or sleep. They may not want to do anything. They may not get out of bed or shower for days.

Heartbreak is like a mortal wound to the soul. A mortal wound to the physical body would lead to death. A mortal wound to the soul would lead to lifelessness in the mind, will, and emotions. Tremendous apathy, low energy, oversleeping, hopelessness, and despair indicate a believer experiencing heartbreak.

Consider Nehemiah after he heard that the survivors in Jerusalem were in "great distress and reproach" and that the wall and gates were in ruins

(Nehemiah 1:3). Nehemiah 1:4 says, "So it was, when I heard these words, that I sat down and wept, and mourned for many days; I was fasting and praying before the God of heaven."

Nehemiah's heart likely broke for his people and beloved city. When mourning, people often suffer sleep and appetite disturbance and problems with concentration and decision–making. They may need to take time away from work to sort through shock, sadness, and loss. Heartbreak can even change how a person looks. Nehemiah 2:1–2 says, "...I took the wine and gave it to the king. Now I had never been sad in his presence before. Therefore, the king said to me, 'Why is your face sad, since you are not sick? This is nothing but sorrow of heart.'" The word "sorrow" in this verse is "roa," meaning to be bad, sad, and injurious. The word "heart" in this verse is "leb" meaning the mind and inner person. When peoples' hearts are broken, they may be forlorn emotionally, which can be evident in their facial expressions.

When Nehemiah was suffering sorrow of heart, it says he prayed. That was a good move. However, when the soul is wounded, believers may not want to pray, read the Bible, or attend church. Scripture shows the reason for this state of affairs. Proverbs 15:13 says, "...by sorrow of the heart the spirit is broken." The word "sorrow" in this verse is "atstsebeth," meaning a wound, hurt, injury, or pain. The word "heart" is "leb," meaning the inner man or mind. The word "spirit" is "ruah" which means wind, spirit, or breath. The word "broken" is "nake," meaning stricken and wounded. This verse says the spirit can be wounded when a believer's soul is injured or in pain. When something is stricken, it is seriously affected by something unpleasant. Heartbreak can entail not only psychological problems but something akin to spiritual flat–lining. Sometimes, in heartbreak, the spirit's heartbeat is arrested. The consequences of heartbreak are no small matter.

Proverbs 17:22 says, "A merry heart does good, like medicine, but a broken spirit dries the bones." This verse shows there are consequences of a broken spirit on the body. A broken spirit causes the source of life in the bones (bones make blood cells) to dry up! Scripture shows us that's what happened to Israel. Ezekiel 37:1–3 says, "The hand of the LORD came upon me and brought me out in the Spirit of the LORD, and set me down in the midst of the valley; and it was full of bones. Then He caused me to pass by them all around, and behold, there were very many in the open valley; and indeed they were very dry. And He said to me, 'Son of man, can these bones live?' So I answered, 'O Lord God, You know.'" What is sad in this picture is that the whole valley was full of dry bones. The nation had been in tough times, and the sorrow of the heart caused their spiritual lives to dry up.

Not surprisingly, the devil may try to break believers' bodies and souls to break their spirits. Believers must be aware of this evil scheme. Satanic attacks are to disable Christians. The devil is trying to hinder God's spiritual kingdom of love. Satan attacked Job's body. Job suffered much grief and upset. The devil wanted Job to pull away from God. Job experienced anguish, but he held onto his faith. Job 2:10 says, "But he said to her [Job's wife], 'You speak as one of the foolish women speaks. Shall we indeed accept good from God, and shall we not accept adversity?' In all this Job did not sin with his lips." Job didn't let sorrow of heart break his spiritual life. We could all learn a lesson from Job.

Heart Revival

After heartbreak, God can revive believers' spirits, souls, and bodies. God revived Israel. Ezekiel 37:4–5 says, "Again He said to me, 'Prophesy to these bones, and say to them, O dry bones, hear the word of the Lord! Thus says the Lord God to these bones: Surely I will cause breath to enter into you, and you shall live.'"

Psalm 85 is a prayer for the LORD to restore and revive hearts. Verse 6 says, "Will You [LORD] not revive us again?" Believers need to pray to God during heartbreaking times. God can revive believers when they can't muster the strength to go on. An image of revival is also found in Acts 3. A man lame from birth had his feet and ankles strengthened. Praise God. Verse 8 says the man "jumped to his feet and began to walk. Then he went with them into the temple courts, walking and jumping and praising God." What a beautiful picture. God restored his body and soul. He who could not serve, now has a walk with a skip in his step. I imagine he touched a lot of lives with his testimony.

Proverbs 18:14 says, "The spirit of a man will sustain him in sickness, but who can bear a broken spirit?" Believers with strong spirits can persist even if they are very ill. However, the soul can be quite wounded and needs encouragement. That is why it is important to speak positively to people who are sick. Social support will minimize the chances of the spirit taking a hit from the soul, and will enliven the soul. Importantly, believers must remember that the soul will never support the spirit. The Word of God is what keeps the spirit strong.

Jacob was named, "supplanter." A supplanter is someone who seizes and usurps. Jacob took Esau's birthright and their father's blessing. Jacob had to leave suddenly to dodge the murderous wrath of his brother. Can you imagine being forced to run for your life? Everything you know is gone. Losing everything all at once is heartbreaking. God later visited Jacob in a dream to give him support and direction. Genesis 28:13–15 says,

> And behold, the LORD stood above it and said: "I am the LORD God of Abraham your father and the God of Isaac; the land on which you lie I will give to you and your descendants. Also your descendants shall be as the dust of the earth; you shall spread abroad to the west and the east, to the north and the south; and in you and in your seed all the families of the earth shall be blessed. Behold, I am with you and will keep you wherever you go, and will bring you back to this land; for I will not leave you until I have done what I have spoken to you."

Jacob was on the run, and God lovingly gave him a map for his life. God gave him something to hold onto during his journey into the unknown. God revived his heart, and he was able to keep going.

After Jesus died, the disciples got down and went back to fishing. They had just spent three years with Jesus learning about spiritual things. Why did they spiritually flatline? It's probably because their souls became crushed. Their leader had been taken captive and killed. They thought their spiritual service was over. When situations dramatically change, it is common for believers to lose sight of their spiritual purposes.

Peter denied Jesus, and his soul became deeply wounded. Jesus went to Peter and spoke words of life to him. After eating with him and the other disciples, Jesus gave him a progressive commission. Start with the new believers, and after growing in the faith, help the mature believers. Jesus gave him direction because he lost his way. John 21:15–17 says,

> So when they had eaten breakfast, Jesus said to Simon Peter, "Simon son of Jonah, do you love Me more than these?" He said to Him, "Yes, Lord; You know that I love You." He said to him, "Feed my lambs." He said to him again a second time, "Simon, son of Jonah, do you love Me?" He said to Him, "Yes, Lord; You know that I love You." He said to him, "Tend My sheep." He said to him the third time, "Simon, son of Jonah, do you love Me?" Peter was grieved because He said to him the third time, "Do you love Me?" And He said to Him. "Lord, You know all things; You know that I love You." Jesus said to him, "Feed My sheep."

Jesus restored Peter after heartbreak so he could function and love again. Sometimes, after heartbreak, it's hard to love people and God. Problems loving are a consequence of having a broken heart. So don't feel bad. Just turn to the Lord. Restoration in love and function is what God can do for all believers.

Prayer Point: Father, please heal the broken places in my heart.

CHAPTER 13 KEY POINTS
Heartbreak

- ❖ When life circumstances crush believers' souls and they cannot function, they are now experiencing heartbreak.
- ❖ In heartbreak, believers often can't even do the basics.
- ❖ Heartbreak is like a mortal wound to the soul.
- ❖ Tremendous apathy, low energy, oversleeping, hopelessness, and despair can be a sign that a believer is experiencing heartbreak.
- ❖ Heartbreak can even change how a person looks.
- ❖ When the soul is wounded, believers may not want to pray, read the Bible, or attend church.
- ❖ Proverbs 15:23 says, "...by sorrow of the heart the spirit is broken."
- ❖ Heartbreak can entail not only psychological problems but something akin to spiritual flat–lining.
- ❖ A broken spirit causes the source of life in the bones to dry up!
- ❖ The devil may try to break believers' bodies and souls to break their spirits.
- ❖ After heartbreak, God can revive believers' spirits, souls, and bodies.
- ❖ Social support will minimize the chances of the spirit taking a hit from the soul, and will enliven the soul.
- ❖ Believers must remember that the soul will never support the spirit. The Word of God is what keeps the spirit strong.
- ❖ When situations dramatically change, it is common for believers to lose sight of their spiritual purposes.
- ❖ Jesus restored Peter after heartbreak so he could function again.
- ❖ Sometimes, after heartbreak, it's hard to love people and God.
- ❖ Problems loving are a consequence of having a broken heart.

CHAPTER 13 STUDY QUESTIONS
Heartbreak

1. Define heartbreak.

2. Name 3 signs that a believer's soul is in heartbreak.

3. Is heartbreak is like a mortal wound to the soul? Yes No

4. Can a broken soul affect a believer's spiritual life? Yes No

5. Describe what may have caused Israel to become a valley of spiritual dry bones.

6. Does Satan aim to break believer's bodies and souls to break their spirits? Yes No

7. What does God do to treat heartbreak?

_____
_____
_____
_____

CHAPTER 14

Heart Abuse

For My yoke is easy and My burden is light.
—Matthew 11:30

Heart abuse is a condition that is self–inflicted. Imagine a very capable believer who makes a mistake. Maybe that believer has a chronic sin problem or a character flaw that keeps causing issues. Perhaps that person is facing an impossible situation. Now imagine that believer berating and putting themselves down repeatedly. The believer ends up feeling miserable and worthless. Such mistreatment is heart abuse in a nutshell.

Believers can feel guilty about poor behavior. Bad feelings when a person does wrong are normal. In heart abuse, believers spend much time and energy tearing apart different aspects of their lives and character. In heart abuse, the negativity is extreme and can border on self–hate. Any misstep may fuel the personal attack. It is as if believers take a black marker and color different aspects of themselves black. The darkness and negativity inside a believer can affect various parts of their life. Believers may not only feel terrible about themselves but circumstances and other people may appear terrible as well. Hope can exit the heart. Doubt, depression, fear, and low self–esteem may predominate.

Believers abusing their hearts are not caring for them but damaging them. I knew a woman who was beautiful inside and out. She would give a lot of time to meaningful causes and would often be praying for someone or helping them with a problem. Her life was positive and fruitful, except for her work. There was a team of people she had to supervise who were mean, irresponsible, and lazy. She tried everything to motivate them but to no avail. She prayed about the matter, but things just kept getting worse. When I saw this woman, she would talk about all her problems at work. She seemed miserable because of what she was doing to herself. Mentally, she viewed every problem as her fault. If someone was late, she thought she kept them too late the night before. If someone did not finish an assignment, she blamed herself. There was nothing positive she could say about her work. When people continually have a "negative forecast" about an area of their life, that can suggest heart abuse. Someone suffering heart abuse may "awfulize" and make a life domain (e.g., work, relationship, homelife) appear bleak.

Heart abuse is common. I've had many people come in for psychotherapy with a long list of things they dislike about themselves and a short list of things they like about themselves. And often, they didn't believe the positive things about themselves. Rooting out heart abuse is essential, but it is not an easy task. Tendencies to nitpick and find fault can become deeply ingrained. Unhealthy childhood family dynamics, negative friends, or unreasonable life goals can usher in heart abuse.

Consider Peter. He denied that he knew Jesus three times. He had professed that he would never leave him. Jesus even warned him that he would do that to Him. Imagine the psychological upset that must have followed. It doesn't say Peter beat himself up. It seems reasonable to imagine that he did. Luke 22:60–62 says, "But Peter said, 'Man, I do not know what you are saying!' Immediately while he was still speaking, the rooster crowed. And the Lord turned and looked at Peter. Then Peter remembered the word of the Lord, how He had said to him, 'Before the rooster crows, you will deny Me three times.' So Peter went out and wept bitterly." I imagine Peter was consumed with painful thoughts. Bitter tears come from a deeply grieved and distressed heart. I wonder if Peter thought he had to be perfect to serve the Lord. Perfectionism is one condition that can set up heart abuse.

To counter heart abuse, believers must seek to understand and internalize their position in Christ. Believers are righteous in Christ. (2nd

Corinthians 5:21 "For He made Him who knew no sin to be sin for us, that we might become the righteousness of God in Him.") Apart from Christ, believers are not in right standing with God. The Bible teaches that believers' "righteousnesses are like filthy rags" (Isaiah 64:6). Initially, I didn't understand this Scripture. I wondered how a good deed was not righteous. This verse makes more sense when believers compare good deeds to God's holiness (He's never sinned). Believers can do something nice outwardly, but the motive or intent is sometimes corrupt.

Righteousness is a gift believers must continually draw from. Romans 5:17 says, "For if by the one man's offense death reigned through the one, much more those who receive abundance of grace and of the gift of righteousness will reign in life through the One, Jesus Christ." Those who trust in God and continually receive the gift of righteousness will have less risk of heart abuse. Being able to say, "I am righteous," even when a mistake is made, is essential for minimizing the risk of heart abuse.

Prayer Point: Father, help me to be merciful with myself when I make a mistake or fall short.

CHAPTER 14 KEY POINTS
Heart Abuse

- ❖ Heart abuse is condition which is self–inflicted.
- ❖ In heart abuse, believers spend much time and energy tearing apart different aspects of their lives and character.
- ❖ In heart abuse, the negativity is extreme and can border on self–hate.
- ❖ Believers abusing their hearts are not caring for them.
- ❖ When a person continually has a "negative forecast," that can suggest heart abuse.
- ❖ Someone suffering heart abuse may "awfulize" and make everything appear bleak.
- ❖ Tendencies to nit pick and find fault can become deeply ingrained.
- ❖ Unhealthy childhood family dynamics, negative friends, or unreasonable life goals can usher in heart abuse.
- ❖ Perfectionism is one condition that can set up heart abuse.
- ❖ Being able to say, "I am righteous" even when a mistake is made is an important practice for minimizing the risk of heart abuse.

CHAPTER 14 STUDY QUESTIONS
Heart Abuse

---

1. Define heart abuse.

   _____
   _____
   _____
   _____

2. Is heart abuse self–inflicted? Yes No

3. Can heart abuse border on self–hate? Yes No

4. List two signs of heart abuse.

   _____
   _____
   _____
   _____

5. Is routing out heart abuse an easy task? Yes No

6. Name four factors that can usher in heart abuse.

   _____
   _____
   _____
   _____

7. Describe how perfectionism can contribute to heart abuse.

   _____
   _____
   _____
   _____

8. Can understanding believers' positions in Christ help reduce heart abuse? Yes No

9. Can saying, "I am righteous in Christ" after an error counter heart abuse? Yes No

CHAPTER 15

Deceived Heart

He feeds on ashes; A deceived heart has turned him aside;
And he cannot deliver his soul, nor say, "Is there not a lie in my right hand?"
—Isaiah 44:20

Have you ever been deceived? You probably were but didn't know it. That's the nature of deception. It's hard to detect. When believers are deceived, it means that there was an intentional misleading, and they have now adopted as truth something false. When people preach or teach lies (e.g., false prophets and teachers), they act as deceivers.

When the heart is deceived, a person will get turned in the wrong direction. Isaiah 44:20 says, "...a deceived heart has turned him aside..." It's a picture of someone going one way, but because of the deception in the heart, that person is now going in a different direction. We could say someone gets off course because of a lie or half–truth. When it comes to discipleship in the Body of Christ, this would be a big problem. Can you imagine shepherding someone who disagrees with what you are saying? It would be a frustrating experience. Amos 3:3 says, "Can two walk together, unless they are agreed?" The answer is probably not. Sooner or later, one person will want to go in one direction, and the other will want to go in another.

Deception has been around since the Garden of Eden. Study the interaction between the serpent and Eve. The devil used specific words to get Eve to doubt God and believe something untrue. Genesis 3:1–5 says,

> Now the serpent was more cunning than any beast of the field which the LORD God had made. And he said to the woman, "Has God indeed said, 'You shall not eat of every tree of the garden'?" And the woman said to the serpent, "We may eat the fruit of the trees of the garden; but of the fruit of the tree which is in the midst of the garden, God has said, 'You shall not eat it, nor shall you touch it, lest you die.'" Then the serpent said to the woman, "You will not surely die. For God knows that in the day you eat of it your eyes will be opened, and you will be like God, knowing good and evil.'"

The devil tries to cast doubt on what God told Eve ("Has God indeed said") and blatantly tells her what she heard was not true ("You will not surely die"). How awful! No wonder the devil was cast out of heaven.

If you don't know about the devil's nature, you may wonder why he would act in such a way towards Eve. The devil is not trying to deceive Eve to get something out of it. His whole nature is corrupt. John 8:44 says, "You are of your father the devil, and the desires of your father you want to do. He was a murderer from the beginning, and does not stand in the truth, because there is no truth in him. When he speaks a lie, he speaks from his own resources, for he is a liar and the father of it." Believers must be wary of the devil's wiles because he wants to cause division between God and man. Second Corinthians 11:3 says, "But I fear, lest somehow, as the serpent deceived Eve by his craftiness, so your minds may be corrupted from the simplicity that is in Christ."

Besides the devil's attempts to corrupt believers' thinking, believers can adopt false ideas independently. Galatians 6:3 says, "For if anyone thinks himself to be something, when he is nothing, he deceives himself." Most people have, at one time or another, believed something that wasn't true, maybe due to pride or lack of understanding.

James 1:22 says, "But be doers of the word, and not hearers only, deceiving yourselves." Sometimes, a believer can know a lot of Bible verses. That doesn't mean that person is spiritual. Hearers only of the Word of God are deceived. They are not spiritual. When believers incorporate the Word of God into their lives and do it, then they are spiritual.

Just because believers have peace about something does not mean they aren't deceived. A believer may have peace in the flesh but not in the spirit. Galatians 5:16 says, "I say then: Walk in the Spirit and you shall not fulfill the lust of the flesh." The flesh is the fallen nature that lives for temporary things of the physical world. It can feel good to fulfill the desires of the flesh, but deep down, believers' spirits would lack peace. For example, a young believer may sleep around because his friends act that way. That person may feel okay about what he is doing in his mind and justifies it by saying, "Everyone is doing it." But his spirit would be grieved.

It's crucial to gain discernment to minimize the risk of deception. When the spirit is made new, it can now interact with God. But even with the Holy Spirit, a believer can believe and act in error. Just think about how many mistakes you made after receiving the Holy Spirit. Sometimes, believers think they are following the Holy Spirit but maybe following logic or fleshly desires. Believers must know spiritual laws. Galatians 6:7 says, "Do not be deceived, God is not mocked; for whatever a man sows, that he will also reap." So, what a person does will definitely come full circle. To believe it won't happen would be self-deception. Bottomline. To guard against deception, believers must know and fully accept God's Word as Truth.

Prayer Point: Father, bring to light any deception that may be bringing confusion or darkness to my heart.

CHAPTER 15 KEY POINTS
Deceived Heart

- ❖ When believers are deceived, it means that there was an intentional misleading, and they have now adopted as truth something false.
- ❖ When people preach or teach lies (e.g., false prophets and teachers), they act as deceivers.
- ❖ When the heart is deceived, a person will get turned in the wrong direction.
- ❖ Amos 3:3 says, "Can two walk together, unless they are agreed?"
- ❖ Deception has been around since the garden of Eden.
- ❖ The devil used specific words to try to get Eve to doubt God and believe something that wasn't true.
- ❖ Believers need to be wary of the devil's wiles because he wants to cause division between God and man.
- ❖ Besides the devil's attempts to corrupts believers' thinking, believers can adopt false ideas independently.
- ❖ Hearers only of the Word of God are deceived.
- ❖ Just because believers have peace about something does not mean they aren't deceived.
- ❖ It's so important to gain discernment to minimize the risk of deception.
- ❖ Galatians 6:7 says, "Do not be deceived, God is not mocked; for whatever a man sows, that he will also reap."
- ❖ To guard against deception, believers need to know God's Word.

CHAPTER 15 STUDY QUESTIONS
Deceived Heart

1. What does it mean to be deceived?

   _____
   _____
   _____
   _____

2. Can deception in the heart cause a person to get off course? Yes No

3. Describe the deception that occurred in the Garden of Eden.

   _____
   _____
   _____
   _____

4. Is the devil's whole nature corrupt? Yes No

5. List one false belief you thought was true.

   _____
   _____
   _____
   _____

6. Are hearers only of the Word of God deceived? Yes No

7. Does peace in the mind means someone is not deceived? Yes No

8. How can discernment help minimize the risk of deception?

_____
_____
_____
_____

16
CHAPTER

Heart–bound

But his wife looked back behind him, and she became a pillar of salt.
—Genesis 19:26

When believers are heart–bound, part or all of their hearts are devoted to something. This can indicate a determination to go in a particular direction, which may or may not be in a person's best interest. When believers are heart–bound, it is like they are in a trap or tied up with ropes. Believers who are heart–bound have a lack of freedom and are suffering constraints. Being heart–bound is a dangerous condition. Why, you may ask? Consider the fate of those in the Bible who were heart–bound.

Lot and his wife were likely heart–bound. Their hearts were bound to something related to Sodom. Genesis 19:15-16 says, "When the morning dawned, the angels urged Lot to hurry, saying, 'Arise, take your wife and your two daughters who are here, lest you be consumed in the punishment of the city.' And while he lingered, the men took hold of his hand, his wife's hand, and the hands of his two daughters, the LORD being merciful to him, and they brought him out and set him outside the city." The word "lingered" in this verse is "mahah" which means "to delay, tarry, and hesitate." The angels warned of imminent destruction, but Lot was not getting a move on. Why? Perhaps his heart was bound. Genesis 19:17 says, "So it came to pass, when they had brought them outside, that he [an angel] said, 'Escape for your life! Do not look behind you nor stay anywhere in the plain. Escape to the mountains, lest you be destroyed.'" Lot, his wife, and two daughters were brought outside the city and told to run or die. That's a frightening directive. It's hard to imagine anyone not complying. Lot's wife looked back. Perhaps the city got in her heart. Maybe she was torn as they were fleeing and wanted one more glimpse of what she was leaving behind. We all know the consequences of her heart condition. She lost her life. She became a pillar of salt.

Achan's heart was bound to things. He took money and clothing when it was forbidden. The cost of his heart condition was the death of everyone in his family, including himself. Joshua 7:11 says, "Israel has sinned, and they have also transgressed My covenant which I commanded them. For they have even taken some of the accursed things, and have both stolen and deceived; and they have also put it among their own stuff." Achan took something that would come in between himself and God. It was a very poor decision. Obey God or pursue things? He chose things. Such a decision seemed to stem from Achan's deep desire to possess.

Esau was heart-bound to the present and comfort. One day, he was working and became hungry. He sold his birthright for a bowl of soup. Esau seemed to be governed by his stomach. Philippians 3:19 says, "Whose end is destruction, whose god is their belly, and whose glory is in their shame – who set their mind on earthly things." In this generation, there is a group of people whose god is their belly. They call themselves "foodies." Such people live each day for their next delicious meal. They may not know it, but they are in a kind of prison.

Solomon's heart was bound to women. He had hundreds of wives, as well as princesses and concubines. First Kings 11:1–4 says,

> But King Solomon loved many foreign women, as well as the daughter of Pharoah: women of the Moabites, Ammonites, Edomites, Sidonians, and Hittites —from the nations of whom the LORD had said to the children of Israel, 'You shall not intermarry with them, nor they with you. Surely they will turn away your hearts after their gods.' Solomon clung to these in love. And he had seven hundred wives, princesses, and three hundred concubines;

and his wives turned away his heart. For it was so, when Solomon was old, that his wives turned his heart after other gods; and his heart was not loyal to the LORD his God, as was the heart of his father David.

How sad. David, a man after God's own heart (Acts 13:22), had a son who did not have the same heart attitude. The word "loyal" in verse 4 is the word "shalem" which means "complete, safe, and at peace." Solomon did not find completeness and peace with God. Instead, he chose to pursue people rather than God to meet his needs. Solomon was a very blessed person (2nd Chronicles 9:22, "So King Solomon surpassed all the kings of the earth in riches and wisdom.") However, his life shows us that a person can go astray even amid great blessings from God.

Judas' heart was bound to money. John 12:4–6 says, "But one of His disciples, Judas Iscariot, Simon's son, who would betray Him said, 'Why was this fragrant oil not sold for three hundred denarii and given to the poor?' This he said, not that he cared for the poor, but because he was a thief, and had the money box; and he used to take what was put in it." I wonder if Judas asked to be in charge of the money box because he wanted to steal from it or if he was put in charge of the money and was tempted to steal. Regardless, Judas was a thief. His heart was overly attached to money. First Timothy 6:10 says, "For the love of money is a root of all kinds of evil…" Believers need to beware of the love of money lest their hearts become bound by it.

Prayer Point: Father, please set free any parts of my heart that are bound.

CHAPTER 16 KEY POINTS
Heart–bound

- When believers are heart–bound, part or all of their heart is devoted to something.
- When believers are heart–bound, it's like they are in a trap or tied up with ropes.
- Believers who are heart–bound have a lack of freedom and are suffering constraints.
- Being heart–bound is a dangerous condition.
- Lot and his wife were heart–bound. Their hearts were bound to something related to Sodom.
- Achan's heart was bound to things. He took money and clothing when it was forbidden.
- Esau was heart–bound to the present and comfort.
- Esau seemed to be governed by his stomach.
- Solomon's heart was bound to women.
- Solomon did not find completeness and peace with God.
- Judas' heart was bound to money.
- Believers need to beware of the love of money lest their hearts become bound by it.

CHAPTER 16 STUDY QUESTIONS
Heart–bound

1. What does it mean to be heart–bound.

2. Can a believer's heart be partially bound to something? Yes No

3. If believers are heart–bound, can it be like they are constrained? Yes No

4. Describe how Lot's wife was heart–bound.

5. What led Achan's heart to be bound?

6. Esau was bound to the _____ and _____.

7. What was the root cause of Solomon being heart–bound to so many women?

_____
_____
_____
_____

CHAPTER 17

A Double Heart

They speak idly everyone with his neighbor;
with flattering lips and a double heart they speak.
—Psalm 12:2

A double heart means a heart with a heart. It's like having two people in one mind with different opinions. One heart thinks one way, and the other heart thinks differently. It's an annoying split associated with much dissonance. I've seen this in practice many times. One man came in for couples counseling with his girlfriend of 6 years. They were having trouble moving forward and pointed fingers at him. While interviewing the man, it became clear that he had strong feelings for his current girlfriend and respected her very much. However, I asked if he still loved his ex–girlfriend, and he said, "Absolutely." I was stunned. The current girlfriend just sighed. The man wanted to be with his current girlfriend, but at the same time, he was still seeing himself with his ex–girlfriend. He had two hearts. Obviously, the couple could not move forward until he dealt with his heart issue.

Psalm 12:2 says, "They speak idly everyone with his neighbor; with flattering lips and a double heart they speak." "Heart" in this verse is the word "leb," which means the inner man or mind. Having a double heart has to do with the soul. A flatterer is someone who praises but often insincerely. Saying one thing externally and believing something else internally suggests double-heartedness. Christians can be double-hearted. Consider a believer who enjoys attending church but deep down thinks religion is a crutch. Or believers may say, "God is my shepherd," but in their hearts, they may not intend to follow Him.

James 1:6–8 says, "But let him ask in faith, with no doubting, for he who doubts is like a wave of the sea driven and tossed by the wind. For let not that man suppose that he will receive anything from the Lord; he is a double-minded man, unstable in all his ways." "Double-minded" in this verse is the word "dipsychos," meaning two minds. When believers have two minds, they fluctuate from one opinion to another and may never solidly land on one.

When a believer is double-minded, there is a war within. I met a spiritual man once who was double-minded. This man had been a pastor at a church before it closed down due to dwindling numbers. This person loved to read the Bible out loud and talk about it. He said he believed the Word of God was true and all His promises were "yes and amen" (2nd Corinthians 1:20 "For all the promises of God in Him are Yes, and in Him Amen, to the glory of God through us"). However, he didn't seem to believe the Word when he became sick. When I asked him if he asked God to heal him, he just stared at me. I handed him a booklet full of scriptures about how God is our healer. I pointed out Exodus 15:26 "…If you diligently heed the voice of the Lord your God and do what is right in His sight, give ear to His commandments and keep all His statutes, I will put none of the diseases on you which I have brought on the Egyptians. For I am the Lord who heals you." I shared Psalm 103:2-3 which says, "Bless the LORD, O my soul, and forget not all His benefits: Who forgives all your iniquities, Who heals all your diseases." I could almost hear the words bouncing off the doubting part of his heart. Having faith-based thoughts and doubt-based thoughts can suggest a double heart. The two are like oil and water. They will never mix.

James 4:4 says, "Adulterers and adulteresses! Do you not know that friendship with the world is enmity with God? Whoever therefore wants to be a friend of the world makes himself an enemy with God." Being a friend of the world and of God would reflect a double heart because many worldly things go against the standards of God.

A DOUBLE HEART

James 4:7–10 says, "Therefore submit to God. Resist the devil and he will flee from you. Draw near to God and He will draw near to you. Cleanse your hands, you sinners; and purify your hearts, you double-minded. Lament and mourn and weep! Let your laughter be turned to mourning and your joy to gloom. Humble yourselves in the sight of the Lord and He will lift you." Believers can't open their minds to the devil's ideas and God's thoughts. When believers think wrongly, they will act wrongly. When believers are double-minded, their hearts need to be purified. One way of thinking has to go. Believers must diligently examine and remove conflicting mindsets, lest double-mindedness set it.

Prayer Point: Father, search my heart and reveal and heal any double heartedness.

CHAPTER 17 KEY POINTS
A Double Heart

- A double heart means a heart with a heart. It's like having two people in one mind with different opinions.
- Psalm 12:2 says, "They speak idly everyone with his neighbor; with flattering lips and a double heart they speak."
- Saying one thing externally and believing something else internally suggests double–heartedness.
- James 1:6–8 says, "But let him ask in faith, with no doubting, for he who doubts is like a wave of the sea driven and tossed by the wind. For let not that man suppose that he will receive anything from the Lord; he is a double–minded man, unstable in all his ways."
- When believers have two minds, they will vacillate from one opinion to another and may never solidly land on one.
- When a believer is double–minded, there is a war within.
- Having faith–based thoughts and doubt–based thoughts can suggest a double heart.
- Being a friend of the world and of God would reflect a double heart because many worldly things go against the standards of God.
- Believers can't open their mind to the devil's ideas and God's thoughts.
- When believers think wrongly they will act wrongly.
- When believers are double minded, their hearts need to be purified.
- Believers need to be diligent in examining and removing conflicting mindsets, lest double mindedness set it.

CHAPTER STUDY 17 STUDY QUESTIONS
A Double Heart

1. What is a double heart?

2. Write out Psalm 12:2 and explain it.

3. Would saying one thing externally and believing something else internally suggest double–heartedness? Yes No

4. What is the Greek word for "double–minded" in James 1:8 and what does it mean?

5. Name one common area of double mindedness.

6. Would having strong faith–based thoughts and doubt–based thoughts at the same time reflect double–mindedness? Explain your answer.

_____
_____
_____
_____

7. Double–mindedness needs to be taken seriously. Yes No

18
CHAPTER

Hard Heart

And the Lord said to Moses, "When you go back to Egypt, see that you do all those wonders before Pharaoh which I have put in your hand. But I will harden his heart, so that he will not let the people go.
–Exodus 4:21

Believers with a hard heart can be unfeeling, pitiless, unsympathetic, and bitter. Pharoah had a hard heart. He repeatedly would not consider the request of the people of Israel to go and worship God. Exodus 7:3 says, "And I will harden Pharoah's heart, and multiply My signs and My wonders in the land of Egypt." Interestingly, the LORD says that he would harden Pharoah's heart so that He could demonstrate His power. Sometimes, a person's heart is hardened so that God's purposes can be accomplished.

When someone's heart is hard, it can become dull and insensitive. Matthew 13:15 says, "For the hearts of this people have grown dull. Their ears are hard of hearing. And their eyes they have closed. Lest they should see with their eyes and hear with their ears. Lest they should understand with their hearts and turn, so that I should heal them." The word "dull" in this verse is "pachuno," meaning to thicken, fatten, and become insensitive. It suggests someone who is not able to sense things accurately. It's like a person who can't see or hear well. Without good input, it's hard to make good decisions. Imagine someone trying to drive with feeble vision. That person may hit the curb, parked cars, or anything near the road.

A hard heart is like a closed door – nothing gets in or out. Consider the wayside in the parable of the sower. Matthew 13:3–4 says, "Then He spoke many things to them in parables, saying: 'Behold, a sower went out to sow. And as he sowed, some seed fell by the wayside; and the birds came and devoured them.'" Seeds falling by the wayside often don't go into the soil. They rest on the surface. That's why the birds can see and eat it. It reminds me of times I've been out evangelizing. I've met people who act like what I said went in one ear and out the other. It's like it didn't register at all. When this happens, I sometimes wonder if I am dealing with a hard-hearted person. Matthew 13:19 teaches, "When anyone hears the word of the kingdom, and does not understand it, then the wicked one comes and snatches away what was sown in his heart. This is he who received seed by the wayside." Jesus teaches that the devil comes and steals the Word when people don't grasp it. Knowing this, we could expect this to happen during evangelism encounters because some people have no knowledge of the Word of God.

There is another type of hardness of heart revealed in Matthew 13. Verse 5–6 says, "Some fell on stony places, where they did not have much earth; and they immediately sprang up because they had no depth of earth. But when the sun was up they were scorched, and because they had no root they withered away." Seeds, soil, and stones are not a good gardening combination. Stones will block seeds from rooting in the soil and may stop a young plant from springing up. Stony places in the heart are treacherous because they are hidden and present dangers to a believer's spiritual growth. A stone in the heart might be an ingrained belief, attitude, or a soul wound. I've met many people who wouldn't receive encouraging words about God's love. People have angrily said, "God doesn't love the world. Look at how many people are suffering and dying every day." Or, "If God loved me so much, why did he let all these bad things happen to me." Their negative beliefs (like stones) keep them from receiving the truth.

About the stony places, Matthew 13:20–21 says, "But he who received the seed on stony places, this is he who hears the word and immediately receives it with joy; yet he has no root in himself, but endures only for a while. For when tribulation or persecution arises because of the word, immediately he stumbles." Jesus teaches that the stones in believers' hearts can keep the Word of God from being deeply planted. The Word carries so little weight when tests and trials come that it doesn't get believers far in dealing with problems. An example would be a believer who says that God will provide but then doesn't ask God for help after losing a job. Rather than asking for another job and standing in faith, that person worries nonstop. Something is blocking this harvest. Could it be that the person doesn't believe in the power of prayer? Maybe the person is bitter and offended. Rather than believing God, they may be thinking, "If God is my provider, why am I jobless?" Either way, "stony places" in the heart may keep a person from really believing and holding onto God's Word.

Ananias seemed to have a hard heart in the area of giving. He didn't want to share. He wanted money from a sale for his use. Acts 5:1–4 says,

> But a certain man named Ananias, with Sapphira his wife, sold a possession. And he kept back part of the proceeds, his wife also being aware of it, and brought a certain part and laid it at the apostles' feet. But Peter said, 'Ananias, why has Satan filled your heart to lie to the Holy Spirit and keep back part of the price of the land for yourself? While it remained, was it not your own? And after it was sold, was it not in your own control? Why have you conceived this thing in your heart? You have not lied to men but to God.'

Ananias's hard heart led him to hoard money and to lie about it. Notice Peter said "Why has Satan filled your heart to lie to the Holy Spirit and keep back part of the price of the land for yourself." This verse shows us that demonic voices may have hardened Ananias's heart against following God's ways.

Job endured tremendous loss, suffering, and undeserved reproach from his friends. Job's contentiousness with God suggests a hardening of heart. Job 10:1–2 says, "My soul loathes my life; I will give free course to my complaint, I will speak in the bitterness of my soul. I will say to God,

'Do not condemn me; Show me why You contend with me.'" Job wanted answers. Ultimately, he realized he needed to trust God for who He is – our loving, caring Creator with a perfect plan for everyone's lives. Job realizes his error in making demands of God. He became contrite and repentant and softened his heart.

Prayer Point: Father, please soften the hard places in my heart.

CHAPTER 18 KEY POINTS
Hard Heart

- ❖ Believers with a hard heart can be unfeeling, pitiless, unsympathetic, and/or bitter.
- ❖ Sometimes a person's heart is hardened so that God's purposes can be accomplished (e.g., Pharaoh).
- ❖ When someone's heart is hard, it can become dull and insensitive.
- ❖ A hard heart is like a closed door – nothing gets in or out.
- ❖ Jesus teaches that the devil comes and steals the Word when people don't grasp it.
- ❖ Stony places in the heart are treacherous because they are hidden and present dangers to a believer's spiritual growth.
- ❖ A "stone" in the heart might be an ingrained belief, attitude, or even a wound.
- ❖ Jesus teaches that the stones in believers' hearts can keep the Word of God from being deeply planted.
- ❖ Ananias had a hard heart in the area of giving. He didn't want to share.
- ❖ A hard heart led Ananias to hoard money and to lie about it.
- ❖ Demonic voices may have hardened Ananias's heart against following God's ways.
- ❖ Job's contentiousness with God suggests a hardening of heart.

CHAPTER 18 STUDY QUESTIONS
Hard Heart

1. How might a person with a hard heart present?

2. Why did God harden Pharoah's heart?

3. Is dullness and insensitivity qualities of a hard heart? Yes No

4. Describe what it might feel like to minister to someone with a hard heart.

5. Describe the wayside and stony places in the parable of the soils and how these conditions may be related to hardness of heart.

6. In what way did Ananias have hardness of heart?

7. What about Job's experience set him up to have contentiousness and hardness of heart?

CHAPTER 19

Fearful Heart

Say to those who are fearful–hearted, "Be strong, do not fear! Behold, your God will come with vengeance, with the recompense of God; He will come and save you."
–Isaiah 35:4

Fear is an unpleasant emotion caused by believing someone or something is dangerous or a threat. Fear can be paralyzing. The physical symptoms of fear can be overwhelming (e.g., racing heart, shakiness, sweating, upset stomach). In the world we live in today, it's hard to imagine living without fear. There are bills to be paid, unexpected life events, massive work stresses, family crises, and more. Turn on the news. Fearful thoughts and feelings sometimes immediately arise.

Past or present situations can trigger a person to have a fearful heart. Imagine being raised in a home with frequent verbal and physical violence. Imagine having neighbors who were critical and threatening and had rigid ideologies and judgmental attitudes. Fear might become the norm.

Proverbs 12:25 says, "Anxiety in the heart of man causes depression, but a good word makes it glad." "Anxiety" in this verse is the word "deagah" which means fear, anxious care, heaviness, or sorrow. "Causes depression" is the word "shachah" which means to weigh down. "Heart" in this verse is the word "leb" meaning inner man, mind, will, or soul." So when someone is in anxious fear, the soul gets bogged down. It's like there is an anchor on the soul causing it to drag and feel heavy.

When the heart is full of fear, it can be challenging to be in faith. Imagine having a bad stomachache for months. Suddenly, the stomach pain gets severe. Because of the length and severity of symptoms, a believer may instantly worry rather than believe the truth that "By Jesus' stripes we are healed" (Isaiah 53:5). Bodily symptoms and soul reactions can contribute to fear, which may trump what a person believes.

Fearful-heartedness sometimes occurs in evangelism. God sent believers to preach the gospel to every creature (Mark 16:15). Many facets of evangelism are unknown, which can trigger fear. Believers sometimes fear being in unfamiliar places, talking to strangers, saying something offensive, and not knowing how to answer questions. Believers can also fear rejection, severe backlash, and verbal abuse. Believing people are dangerous or that others have more power and authority can undermine a believer's ministry efforts. When believers fear people, they are mentally making God smaller than people. This way of thinking needs to be revised. Scripture encourages believers to fear God and not man:

Let us hear the conclusion of the whole matter: Fear God and keep His commandments, For this is man's all. (Ecclesiastes 12:13)

And do not fear those who kill the body but cannot kill the soul. But rather fear Him who is able to destroy both soul and body in hell. (Matthew 10:28)

I, even I am He who comforts you. Who are you that you should be afraid of a man who will die, And of the son of a man who will be made like grass? (Isaiah 51:12)

Proverbs 29:25 says, "The fear of man brings a snare, but whoever trusts in the LORD shall be safe." When believers fear people, God says it will bring a snare, a trap, or a lure. When believers are trapped, they can't do what they need to do. When lured away, it's impossible to complete God's will.

Saul had a fear of man. When he was to be declared king before the nation, Saul was found hiding in the luggage. Saul was seemingly dragged into the spotlight. From the beginning, Saul wanted no part in being the king of Israel. When Samuel informs Saul he will be king, Saul doesn't seem to believe it (1 Samuel 9:21). He had been out looking for his father's missing donkeys. When he went home, Saul didn't even tell his family about his anointing (1 Samuel 10:16).

After Saul became king, he continued to have a fear of man. He was given a command by God to destroy everything in a raid. He disobeyed and saved the king of the Amalekites and some animals for sacrifice. Later, Saul admitted to Samuel that he disobeyed God's command because he feared the people (1 Samuel 15:24 "Then Saul said to Samuel, 'I have sinned, for I have transgressed the commandment of the Lord and your words, because I feared the people and obeyed their voice.'") Believers do well in obeying God rather than men.

Peter suffered fear of man. After Jesus had been taken and questioned, Peter denied Him three times. Peter went away in anguish because the fear in his heart was revealed. Later, Peter seems to have overcome the fear of man. First Peter 3:14 says, "But even if you should suffer for righteousness' sake, you are blessed. And do not be afraid of their threats, nor be troubled."

Nicodemus was an influential Jewish ruler who met Jesus after sundown, likely out of fear of man. In the cover of night, Nicodemus may have been minimizing his risk of being discovered talking to Jesus. John 3:1–2 says, "Now there was a man of the Pharisees named Nicodemus, a ruler of the Jews. This man came to Jesus by night and said to him, 'Rabbi, we know that you are a teacher come from God, for no one can do these signs that you do unless God is with him.'"

Galatians 1:10 declares, "For do I now persuade men, or God? Or do I seek to please men? For if I still pleased men, I would not be a bondservant of Christ." Believers should aim to please God, not man, in their daily work and service. Staying mindful of God's presence and willingness to help others can help minimize fearful–heartedness.

Prayer Point: Father, help me to be ever mindful of Your power and presence and to rule over any fear that may try to grip my heart.

CHAPTER 19 KEY POINTS
Fearful Heart

- ❖ Fear is an unpleasant emotion caused by a belief that someone or something is dangerous or a threat.
- ❖ Past and present situations can trigger a person to have a fearful heart.
- ❖ When the heart is full of fear, it can be difficult to be in faith.
- ❖ Bodily symptoms and soul reactions can contribute to fear which may trump what a person believes.
- ❖ Fearful–heartedness sometimes occurs in evangelism.
- ❖ Many facets of evangelism are unknown which can trigger fear.
- ❖ When believers fear people, they are mentally making God smaller than people.
- ❖ Proverbs 29:25 says, "The fear of man brings a snare, but whoever trusts in the LORD shall be safe."
- ❖ Saul had fear of man. When he was to be declared king before the nation, Saul was found hiding in the luggage and seemingly dragged into the spotlight.
- ❖ After Saul became king, he continued to have fear of man.
- ❖ Peter suffered fear of man.
- ❖ Nicodemus was a powerful Jewish ruler who met Jesus after sundown likely out of fear of man.
- ❖ Believers should aim to please God and not man in their daily work and service.
- ❖ Staying mindful of God's presence and willingness to help can help minimize fearful–heartedness.

CHAPTER 19 STUDY QUESTIONS
Fearful Heart

1. Define fear.

2. Can fear be paralyzing? Yes No

3. Name two situations that have provoked fear in your heart.

4. Can fear trump faith? Yes No

5. Name 5 fears associated with evangelism.

6. Write out two Bible verses about how believers are to fear God and not man.

7. What does Proverbs 29:25 ("The fear of man brings a snare") mean?

8. How did King Saul's fear of man manifest?

CHAPTER 20

Heart Block

For what I am doing, I do not understand. For what I will to do, that I do not practice, what I hate, that I do. If, then, I do what I will not to do, I agree with the law that it is good. But now, it is no longer I who do it, but sin that dwells in me. For I know that in me (that is, in my flesh) nothing good dwells; for to will is present with me, but how to perform what is good I do not find. For the good that I will to do, I do not do; but the evil I will not to do, that I practice. Now if I do what I will not to do, it is no longer I who do it, but sin that dwells in me.
—Romans 7:15–20

The physical heart has an electrical system. The sinus node sends signals through the heart regularly to make the heart contract. When the electrical signal that controls the heart is partially or wholly blocked, this is called heart block. This condition affects the heart's ability to pump blood. People may experience fainting, dizziness, shortness of breath, and tiredness with physical heart block. Surgical insertion of a pacemaker to stimulate the heart is one medical intervention for this problem.

The soul can experience heart block. In heart block of the soul, believers want to act a certain way but have trouble doing so. When believers suffer heart block, desires of the heart (e.g., to be nice to someone) don't necessarily appear on the outside. In heart block, something short circuits. Romans 7:15–20 (see top of page 142) outlines believers' struggle to do what they mean to do and not what they don't want to do. It's a baffling condition. One would think that if people want to do something, they would just be able to do it. That is not the case with heart block.

In heart block, something is causing the original intent to be intercepted. Think of a quarterback throwing a pass. He wants his wide receiver to catch the ball, but another player gets in the way. There can be many causes for people's best intentions to be thwarted.

One cause of heart block is offense. Proverbs 18:19 says, "A brother offended is harder to win than a strong city, and contentions are like the bars of a castle." If someone doesn't meet expectations, this sets up the conditions for an offense. With an offense often comes hurt and angry thoughts and feelings. For protection, walls are erected around the heart. With walls around the heart, the flow of love in and out of the heart becomes hindered. This causes symptoms of heart block.

I knew a couple once in which both would go through times of heart block. The young woman was cheated on by her husband for an entire year. When she found out, it was a devastating blow. Her whole world got turned upside down. She would say she wanted to be peaceful and loving towards her husband. Still, she would be verbally violent and cruel right in front of me. She had heart block due to the trauma of being betrayed. At other times, I saw the husband acting similarly. I think he was offended and traumatized by her verbal abuse, so he would suffer heart block and not behave as he wanted to.

Fear can cause heart block. When believers fear, they can get caught up in thoughts that cause emotional distress. Anxious thoughts and dread can be powerful. When the soul is full of fear-filled angst, it can be difficult for the heart's energies of love to flow. The soul's issues block the innermost expressions of the heart. First John 4:18 says, "There is no fear in love; but perfect love casts out fear, because fear involves torment. But he who fears has not been made perfect in love." This verse suggests that when believers are flowing in love, fear can be less of an issue. However, if a heart is wounded and unable to love well, fear can be a problem.

Pride can set up conditions for heart block. When believers are proud, they try to do things in their own wisdom and power. They don't think to rely on God and His strength. Pride especially short circuits the flow of

HEART BLOCK

love from the heart because God will work against someone operating in pride. James 4:6 says, "But He gives more grace. Therefore He says: 'God resists the proud, But gives grace to the humble.'" Imagine trying to move forward and another person holding you back. Pride sets up resistance and can take the wind out of someone's sails. Pride can hinder one's love walk with the Lord.

Sin can also contribute to heart block. Sin separates believers from God and His help. Isaiah 59:1–2 says, "Behold, the LORD's hand is not shortened, that it cannot save; nor His ear heavy that it cannot hear. But your iniquities have separated you from your God; and your sins have hidden His face from you, so that He will not hear." It's always best to keep short accounts with God. The short and long-term effects of sin can be disastrous.

Another cause of heart block is neural programming in the brain. Say a person goes through years of verbal abuse by an alcoholic parent. One part of that person's brain may be wired for avoidance, shut down, defense, and possibly offense. If a person operates from the hardwiring set up by the abuse, trust and love may not readily come forth.

Lack of dreams can be a sign of heart block. Psalm 16:7–8 says, "I will bless the LORD who has given me counsel; My heart also instructs me in the night seasons. I have set the LORD always before me; Because He is at my right hand I shall not be moved." Typically, God will instruct believers while they sleep. So, if believers are not hearing from God at night, it could mean they are suffering heart block.

Prayer Point: Father, please remove anything from my heart that could be blocking the flow of love.

CHAPTER 20 KEY POINTS
Heart Block

- The soul can experience heart block.
- In heart block of the soul, believers want to act a certain way, but have trouble doing so.
- When believers suffer heart block, desires of the heart (e.g., to be nice to someone) don't necessarily appear on the outside.
- In heart block, there is something that is causing the original intent to be intercepted.
- One cause of heart block is offense.
- Proverbs 18:19 says, "A brother offended is harder to win than a strong city, and contentions are like the bars of a castle."
- Fear can cause heart block.
- When the soul is full of fear-filled angst, it can be difficult for the heart's energies of love to flow.
- Pride can set up conditions for heart block.
- Pride especially short circuits the flow of love from the heart because God will work against someone operating in pride.
- Sin can also contribute to heart block. Sin separates believers from God and His help.
- Lack of dreams can be a sign of heart block.

CHAPTER 20 STUDY QUESTIONS
Heart Block

---

1. What is heart block in the soul?

2. In heart block, what is intercepted?

3. Describe how offense causes heart block.

4. Write out 1st John 4:18 and explain the relationship between fear and love.

5. Why are the proud at risk for heart block?

_____

_____

_____

_____

6. When someone is in sin, how can this contribute to heart block?

_____

_____

_____

_____

7. Is it normal of believers to hear from God in dreams? Yes No

21
CHAPTER

Mind–bending

Then it happened one evening that David arose from his bed and walked on the roof of the king's house. And from the roof he saw a woman bathing, and the woman was very beautiful to behold. So David sent and inquired about the woman. And someone said, "Is this not Bathsheba, the daughter of Eliam, the wife of Uriah the Hittite?" Then David sent messengers, and took her; and she came to him, and he lay with her, for she was cleansed from her impurity; and she returned to her house.
–2nd Samuel 11:2–4

When something is mind–bending, it is mind–altering. Mind warping. What a believer sees or hears can be mind–bending. Having an altered mind can lead to egregious outcomes. Consider King David. He saw Bathsheba bathing, and he went on to commit premeditated murder. One would think that David would not have succumbed to what he saw. David was a man after God's heart (Acts 13:22 "And when He had removed him, He raised up for them David as king, to whom also He gave testimony and said, 'I have found David the son of Jesse, a man after My own heart, who will do all my will'"). King David's mistake shows how what is seen can dramatically affect a person's thinking and behavior.

Achan's mind was bent by what he saw. When conquering the land, he saw rich spoils and took some. It seems unbelievable he would do such a thing given the instructions from God not to take any spoils. But his mind was bent. Unfortunately, his actions led to the defeat of a nation at war and the death of his whole family.

What is heard can also significantly affect a person's thinking and behavior. Consider Eve. She listened to the serpent's words (Genesis 3:4: "Then the serpent said to the woman, 'You will not surely die'"), partook of the fruit of the tree of the knowledge of good and evil, and suffered separation from God. Her mind was warped. She was no longer thinking of God's thoughts but what the devil had said to her through the serpent. When believers are told certain things, their minds can be bent.

Think about what happens when two people who don't know each other are in the same situation regularly. Over time, these two people may start to act and think alike. I remember seeing girls in the same classroom all day begin to think and act alike. They would dress alike, use the same slang, and do the same things. Minds can be bent through association.

Folie a deux is a well-known concept in psychiatric literature that involves mind-bending. Folie a deux means "madness shared by two." In this case, delusions are transferred from one person to another. It's considered a rare happening, but it does happen. In this case, one person's mind is bent by the beliefs and thoughts of another. For example, one person may believe the world is going to end by zombie invasion tomorrow. If their close friend also adopted this belief, this would be folie a deux.

Stockholm syndrome likely involves mind-bending. Think about people who are kidnapped and held hostage. They are under intense duress. Their minds are not going to think the way they usually would. In Stockholm syndrome, captors and captives start to think alike. The term originated from a bank hostage situation in which four victims would not testify against their captors in court. One would think that someone held hostage against their will would want to testify against their captors. In this case, none of the hostages wished to testify against the bank robbers. Captives' thoughts are likely bent in response to traumatic circumstances.

Prayer Point: Father, protect me from mind-bending, and heal any parts of my soul that have been bent by what I have seen or heard.

CHAPTER 21 KEY POINTS
Mind–bending

- ❖ When something is mind–bending, it is mind–altering. Mind warping.
- ❖ What a believer sees or hears can be mind–bending.
- ❖ Having an altered mind can lead to egregious outcomes.
- ❖ King David's mistake shows how what is seen can dramatically affect a person's thinking and behavior.
- ❖ Achan's mind was bent by what he saw.
- ❖ What is heard can significantly affect a person's thinking and behavior.
- ❖ When believers are told certain things, their mind can be bent.
- ❖ Minds can be bent through association.
- ❖ Folie a deux is a well known concept in psychiatric literature that seems to involve mind bending.
- ❖ Folie a deux means "madness shared by two."
- ❖ Stockholm syndrome likely involved mind–bending.
- ❖ In Stockholm syndrome, captors and captives start to think alike.
- ❖ Captives' thoughts are likely bent in response to traumatic circumstances.

CHAPTER 21 STUDY QUESTIONS
Mind–bending

1. Describe mind–bending.

2. How was King David's mind altered?

3. What bent Achan's mind?

4. What did Eve hear that warped her mind?

5. Can minds be bent through association? Yes No

6. What does folie a deux mean?

_____
_____
_____
_____

7. How does Stockholm syndrome involve mind–bending?

_____
_____
_____
_____

CHAPTER 22

Heartworm

And I will restore to you the years that the locust hath eaten, the cankerworm, and the caterpiller, and the palmerworm, my great army which I sent among you. KJV.
—Joel 2:25

Heartworms are parasites that live in the heart of an animal and very rarely a person. Heartworms cause damage to the heart and other organs. Heartworms live in another organism, taking up space and nutrients. Heartworms can happen to the soul. A psychological heartworm is when something in the soul takes from it and does not add value. An example of a psychological heartworm might be a negative mindset or core belief. For example, a person might believe they will always fail no matter how hard they try. This belief would dominate a person's thinking, subtracting hope and positive thoughts. A result of a negative mindset can be problems functioning in a particular area and possibly loss of a dream or destiny.

Heartworm is like the worms that ate up the harvest in Joel 2:25 (written above). Interestingly, a cankerworm is a worm that makes tiny holes in the leaves. It doesn't kill the branch immediately, but usually after a few years. A cankerworm puts tremendous stress on trees. Leaves, branches, and roots can be adversely affected. If left untreated, the tree may be so weak and vulnerable after a few years that it can die.

Offense can act as a psychological heartworm. Offense takes away good sentiments (e.g., "I can trust this person" or "This person has my back"). It may damage a person's relationship with someone. Offense doesn't add anything positive to someone's thinking. Instead, it reduces the ability to love and typically blocks communication. If unchecked, an offense can ruin a bond with someone, such as a spouse, colleague, or old friend.

Behaviors stemming from wrong thoughts can act like a heartworm when they hinder believers from reaching their goals. Consider a man entrenched in an affair at work who decides to stop cheating. He blocks the woman's phone number and stops talking to her. These behaviors begin to help him reach his goal of ending an affair. But, a week later, the man has lunch with the woman. Later that night, he texts her and sets a time to see her again. What happened? Perhaps he thought, "Having lunch is not cheating." He doesn't realize that his little indiscretions are setting him up for failure. Unhelpful thoughts ushered in behaviors that sabotaged his progress. This person needs to set firm boundaries in his mind and life. Without them, he is destined to repeat the same problematic behaviors repeatedly.

Heartworm is akin to the "Little foxes that spoil the vines" talked about in the Song of Solomon (Song of Solomon 2:15: "Catch us the foxes, the little foxes that spoil the vines, for our vines have tender grapes."). A little fox is like a heartworm nibbling at a stream of life and causing death. A vine in the Bible can represent a person's relationship with God. Little problems (e.g., doubt, fear, lack of understanding, distrust, pride) can spoil a believer's connection with God. It is so important that believers regularly assess their connectedness to God. Little issues can cause significant rifts.

I had a patient recently with a psychological heartworm. This middle-aged man said he was doing everything possible to ensure he had peace and happiness in life. He worked hard, cared for his home and pets, and would help his friends and parents often. But he said he would "dig holes" and "find fault" with everything he did. He said he would never be satisfied with his reports and messages in his work. He would criticize himself severely when he found typos or errors. At home, nothing was ever clean or organized enough for him. He never felt satisfied with anything. He always felt like he had to buy new things but never felt better. He never thought he was doing enough with his friends and parents or doing something well for them. His thoughts about things were ruining his efforts. He had psychological heartworms robbing him of peace and joy. It was obvious he was doing the best he could. He could never acknowledge the positive. He was miserable and a bit hopeless. Someone who tries hard but negates all their efforts has a psychological heartworm.

Here's a situation that reminded me of heartworm. I was preparing to attend a three–day Christian conference about 5 hours away. The plan was for a close friend and I to discuss a few issues while in the car. However, a mutual friend kept texting about how much he wanted to go and needed a ride. At first, I thought that I had to take the person. I felt like it was the Christian thing to do. But as I prayed about it, I sensed this person was inserting himself into the situation like a "space invader" and "blessing blocker." This situation made me think of heartworm. I couldn't get my mind off the problem and lost my peace. With that person in the car, there could be no working through the issues I wanted to address with my close friend. The extra person (who had mild dementia and multiple medical problems) would stress us out and likely add tension and irritation. Once I realized what was happening, I committed to traveling alone with my friend, and peace returned. Believers need to eradicate anything that robs them of energy and resources.

Prayer Point: Father, identify and eradicate anything affecting my soul that is draining resources, stealing strength, or subtracting life.

CHAPTER 22 KEY POINTS
Heartworm

- ❖ Heartworm can happen to the soul.
- ❖ A psychological heartworm is when something in the soul takes from it and does not add value.
- ❖ An example of a psychological heartworm might be a negative mindset or core belief.
- ❖ Heartworm is like the worms that ate up the harvest in Joel 2:25.
- ❖ Offense can act as a psychological heartworm.
- ❖ Offense doesn't add anything positive to someone's thinking. Rather it reduces the ability to love and typically blocks communication.
- ❖ Behaviors stemming from wrong thoughts can act like a heartworm when they hinder believers from reaching their goals.
- ❖ Heartworm is akin to the "Little foxes that spoil the vines" talked about in the Song of Solomon.
- ❖ Little problems (e.g., doubt, fear, lack of understanding, distrust, pride) can spoil a believer's connection with God if left unchecked.
- ❖ Someone who tries hard, but negates all their efforts has a psychological heartworm.
- ❖ Believers need to eradicate anything that robs them of energy and resources.

CHAPTER 22 STUDY QUESTIONS
Heartworm

1. Define psychological heartworm.

2. How might a negative mindset be like a psychological heartworm?

3. What might be subtracted from an offended person's thinking?

4. How could a wrong thought sabotage a goal?

5. Write out Song of Solomon 2:15 and explain what the "little foxes" do.

_____
_____
_____
_____

6. Describe how a cankerworm can destroy a tree.

_____
_____
_____
_____

CHAPTER 23

Cancer of the Mind

Keep your heart with all diligence, for out of it spring the issues of life
—Proverbs 4:23

A cancer cell is a normal cell that has become abnormal. Normal cells grow, divide, and die. Cancer cells do not act like normal cells. Cancer cells keep multiplying without dying. As a result, they flood the body locally and sometimes systemically.

The mind can have cancer. When the mind has cancer, it is overrun with abnormal beliefs and thoughts. Someone with cancer of the mind intends to think correctly but struggles. In cancer of the mind, the mind becomes plagued with beliefs and thoughts that neither support the person's identity nor reflect their life situation. In cancer of the mind, a person can typically hear from God spiritually. However, their thoughts are so distracting they may not remember what God said.

For example, I met a man with a Master's degree. He had an excellent work ethic, superior intelligence, good interpersonal skills, and generally healthy thoughts and emotions. But when it came to his work, his thoughts appeared disturbed. This man had been trying to leave a job for four years. In his position, he was underpaid, undervalued, lacked fulfillment, and experienced mistreatment from coworkers. He quit twice but quickly unresigned both times. When I talked with him, he had rational reasons for wanting to leave and stay at his job. His thoughts about himself, however, made no sense. He believed he was a terrible employee and thought he would get fired every day. He never thought he was doing a good job. His mind was overrun with fearful and doubt–filled thoughts, and he could not get a handle on them. This man lost two jobs in the past, but not because of anything he had done. The companies just downsized and relocated. I started suspecting cancer of the mind in his case because his thoughts did not fit what I knew about him.

In cancer of the mind, warped unhealthy thoughts crowd out healthy thoughts. People with cancer of the mind may try to eliminate warped ideas, but they keep returning. I met a woman once who constantly feared being sick. Each time we met, she had another physical concern. Over time, I started suspecting cancer of the mind because she never had peace and continually believed she was sick. One week, it was a stomach problem. The following week, it was her muscles. The next week, it was her brain. And on and on. No amount of reassurance ever helped. When someone has cancer of the mind, there seems to be no end to the problematic thinking.

One possible cause of cancer in the mind is fear related to trauma. I met a lady who was terrorized by abusive parents and relatives growing up. Constant criticism and blame happened. She feared being around her family because of the terrible torment they brought. As an adult, this woman is now consumed by fearful thoughts in social situations. Rather than peaceful and friendly thoughts, she suffers upsetting thoughts such as, "What's gonna go wrong today?" "I wonder who will give me a hard time at work?" "I can never think of anything to say, so I won't say anything." Trauma can severely wound the mind, and sometimes, the results are seemingly unending, warped, and unhelpful thoughts. If thoughts are not managed, as Proverbs 4:23 suggests, problems will ensue.

Another cause of cancer of the mind is spiritual. The Bible shows that spirits can insert thoughts into believers' minds. John 13:2 says, "And supper being ended, the devil having already put it into the heart of Judas Iscariot, Simon's son, to betray Him." The word "heart" in this verse is "kardia," meaning character, will, and mind. Satan filled Judas' heart with something evil. He put the idea of betraying Jesus. It wasn't Judas' thought. Here's another biblical example. Acts 5:3 says, "But Peter said, "Ananias, why has Satan filled your heart to lie to the Holy Spirit and keep back part of the price of the land for yourself?" In this case, Satan put a lie in Ananias, and he gave in to it. Thought insertion is real. The next time you have a negative, unrighteous, or evil view that doesn't fit who you are or your life situation, don't accept it. Please do not assume it is your own. Some thoughts can be from evil spirits. It is good practice to compare ideas to the truth of the Bible. It is wise to eliminate beliefs that do not line up with the Word of God.

Prayer Point: Father, reveal the root of any unproductive lines of thinking in my mind, and bring health and healing to my thought life.

CHAPTER 23 KEY POINTS
Cancer of the Mind

- The mind can have cancer.
- When the mind has cancer, it is overrun with abnormal beliefs and thoughts.
- Someone with cancer of the mind intends to think correctly but struggles.
- In cancer of the mind, the mind becomes plagued with beliefs and thoughts that neither support the person's identity nor reflect their life situation.
- In cancer of the mind, a person can typically hear from God spiritually. However, their thoughts are so distracting they may not remember what God said.
- In cancer of the mind, warped unhealthy thoughts crowd out healthy thoughts.
- People with cancer of the mind may try to eliminate warped thoughts, but they keep coming back.
- One possible cause of cancer in the mind is fear related to trauma.
- Trauma can severely wound the mind; sometimes, the results are seemingly unending warped and unhelpful thoughts.
- Another cause of cancer of the mind is spiritual.
- The Bible shows that spirits can insert thoughts into believers' minds.
- Thought insertion is real.
- The next time you have a negative, unrighteous, or evil thought that doesn't fit who you are or your life situation, don't accept it.
- Some thoughts can be from evil spirits.
- It is good practice to compare thoughts to the truth of the Bible.
- It is wise to eliminate thoughts that do not line up with the Word of God.

CHAPTER 23 STUDY QUESTIONS
Cancer of the Mind

---

1. What happens to thoughts in cancer of the mind?

   _____
   _____
   _____
   _____

2. Can someone with cancer of the mind have trouble thinking properly? Yes No

3. In cancer of the mind, the mind becomes _____ with thoughts that neither support the person's identity nor reflect their life situation.

4. What gets crowded out in cancer of the mind?

   _____
   _____
   _____
   _____

5. Describe how trauma may be a precursor to cancer of the mind.

   _____
   _____
   _____
   _____

6. Write out two scriptures that show evil spirits inserting thoughts in peoples' minds.

CHAPTER 24

Cancer of the Heart

But He turned and said to Peter, "Get behind Me, Satan! You are an offense to Me, for you are not mindful of the things of God, but the things of men."
—Matthew 16:23

Within believers is a spiritual landscape. Try to imagine walking on a flat road toward a horizon. You see the road in front of you, the horizon in the distance, and the landscape all around. This kind of landscape is within believers. It's a spiritual landscape that believers can see with their spiritual eyes. Scripture alludes to this landscape. Luke 17:20–21 says, "Now when He was asked by the Pharisees when the kingdom of God would come, He answered them and said, 'The kingdom of God does not come with observation; nor will they say, See here! or See there! For indeed, the kingdom of God is within you.'" The kingdom of God is a spiritual kingdom within believers. Believers have a spiritual landscape in their hearts, whether they know it or not.

In the Old Testament, Israel was led to a physical place, which was to be their Promised Land. Since Jesus' resurrection, the believer's Promised Land is spiritual. The Promised Land is in Christ Jesus. It's spiritual territory that needs to be taken. Just like Israel had to fight giants in the Old Testament, believers must fight spiritual giants to take possession of their land. Believers must overcome spiritual squatters such as spirits of fear, doubt, pride, control, unbelief, and many others. Believers are in a spiritual war and must endure. There can be many spiritual battles. Second Timothy 2:3 says, "You therefore must endure hardship as a good soldier of Jesus Christ."

Cancer of the heart happens when one or more evil spirits have invaded a person's spiritual landscape. A key scripture highlighting this process is in the New Testament. Matthew 12:43–45 says, "When an unclean spirit goes out of a man, he goes through dry places, seeking rest, and finds none. Then he says, 'I will return to my house from which I came.' And when he comes, he finds it empty, swept, and put in order. Then he goes and takes with him seven other spirits more wicked than himself, and they enter and dwell there; and the last state of that man is worse than the first. So shall it also be with this wicked generation." Notice that one evil spirit goes and gets "seven other spirits more wicked." This is not a small increase in numbers. It's a large jump from 1 to 8. Also, the spirits are "more wicked" which underscores another increase in the evil burden. The picture is of someone who goes from a relatively low level of spiritual oppression to much more oppression. That's how it is with cancer in the body. First, there is one mutant cell, but it rapidly replicates, and soon, there are many malignant cells.

Jesus warns about spiritual oppression that gets worse. John 5:14 says, "Afterward Jesus found him in the temple, and said to him, 'See you have been made well. Sin no more, lest a worse thing come upon you.'" Jesus informs the man that while he was healed, future spiritual peace is not guaranteed. Jesus teaches the man that further waywardness will mean more significant spiritual opposition, torment, and suffering. It is dangerous to backslide spiritually.

Cancer of the spirit may not be evident to the oppressed. However, other people can sometimes detect the problem by a person's behavior. Luke 9:55 says, "But He [Jesus] turned and rebuked them [James and John] and said, 'You do not know what manner of spirit you are of.'" James and John asked Jesus if He wanted them to command fire down to consume people who would not receive Him. Jesus said you don't know it, but an evil spirit is affecting you. Rather than flowing in love, these believers were murderous. Even in the presence of God, believers can think and do evil. Oppression by evil spirits is a real thing.

CANCER OF THE HEART

The man of the Gadarenes appeared overrun with evil spirits. Luke 8:30–31 says, "Jesus asked him, saying, 'What is your name?' And he said, 'Legion,' because many demons had entered him. And they begged Him that He would not command them to go out into the abyss." Many demons had entered this man, and he was suffering so much. He was naked, homeless, "often seized" by the evil spirits, and had to be kept "under guard, bound with chains and shackles." (Luke 8:29). A legion was a division in the Roman Army, numbering approximately six thousand. We can surmise that this man's spiritual condition went from bad to worse. Thank goodness Jesus showed up when He did! God delivered this man, and he was free from dreadful spiritual oppression.

One spirit potentially associated with cancer of the heart is "Abaddon." Abaddon is known as the "destroyer." It is a lurking spirit and a territory taker. Abaddon can enter believers when they focus on and speak destructive words such as, "I'm ruined; my life is in shambles; I am a wreck; my life has been destroyed." Speaking destruction will usher in destruction because what a believer decrees will be established (Job 22:28).

Cancer of the heart is different from cancer of the mind. Believers can discern the difference by assessing the effects. With cancer of the mind, thoughts will be adversely affected. A believer will be able to hear from God but, at times, cannot remember what was heard because of the overwhelming number of abnormal thoughts. In cancer of the heart, a believer may have normal ideas but has difficulties hearing from God. Sometimes, a believer may not hear from God at all. In cancer of the heart, it is like a person's spiritual antenna is broken or bent. A person may be open to hearing from God, but one or more spirits interfere. Luke 8:11–12 says, "Now the parable is this: The seed is the word of God. Those by the wayside are the ones who hear; then the devil comes and takes away the word out of their hearts, lest they should believe and be saved." Notice the devil comes and steals the word of God. The message was sent, but the devil robs the believer of the benefit of retaining the Word. It's like the message was erased. At times, believers are not to blame for forgetting the Word of God. Sometimes, the cause is evil spirits affecting the heart.

Prayer Point: Father, please usher in deliverance if I am suffering oppression from evil spirits.

CHAPTER 24 KEY POINTS
Cancer of the Heart

- ❖ Within believers there is a spiritual landscape.
- ❖ Since Jesus' resurrection, the believer's Promised Land is in Him. It's spiritual territory which needs to be taken.
- ❖ Just like Israel had to fight giants in the Old Testament, believers must fight spiritual giants.
- ❖ Cancer of the heart happens when a person's spiritual landscape has been invaded by one or more evil spirits.
- ❖ When an evil spirit is present, a person can have trouble hearing from God.
- ❖ One spirit associated with cancer of the heart is "Abaddon."
- ❖ Abaddon is known as the "destroyer." It is a lurking spirit and a territory taker.
- ❖ Abaddon can enter believers when they focus on and speak destructive words such as, "I'm ruined; my life is in shambles; I am a wreck; my life has been destroyed."
- ❖ Speaking destruction will usher in destruction because what a believer decrees will be established (Job 22:28).
- ❖ Cancer is the heart is different from cancer of the mind.
- ❖ With cancer of the mind, thoughts will be adversely affected.
- ❖ In cancer of the heart, a believer may have normal thoughts, but they have difficulties hearing from God.
- ❖ In cancer of the heart, it is like a person's spiritual antenna is broken or bent. A person may be open to hearing from God, but one or more spirits interfere.

CHAPTER 24 STUDY QUESTIONS
Cancer of the Heart

1. Describe the spiritual landscape within believers' hearts.

2. Where is New Testament believers' Promised Land?

3. Define cancer of the heart.

4. Can a believer have trouble hearing from God with cancer of the heart? Yes No

5. Can believers have a spirit and not know it? (Explain referring to Luke 9:55)

6. Describe Abaddon and how this spirit affects believers.

_____
_____
_____
_____

7. What is the difference between cancer of the mind and cancer of the heart?

_____
_____
_____
_____

8. If someone can't hear from God, what could this mean? (refer to John 10:27)

_____
_____
_____
_____

CHAPTER 25

Heart Constrictors

And now abide faith, hope, love, these three; but the greatest of these is love.
—1 Corinthians 13:13

Heart constrictors restrict believers from pouring love from their hearts. As a tourniquet around the arm reduces blood flow, heart constrictors limit love's flow. According to Romans 5:5, believers have "the love of God" in their hearts. That's not the problem. It's getting love into relationships. A healthy heart pours out love. A heart that cannot release love is sometimes constricted. There are many causes of heart constriction. Below are a few common heart constrictors and a Biblical meditation to combat the constrictor.

Cares

When believers try to carry and handle every problem and care, their hearts can get bogged down. In these circumstances, it can be challenging for the heart to function normally.

REMEDY: 1 Peter 5:6–7 "Therefore humble yourselves under the mighty hand of God, that He may exalt you in due time, casting all your care upon Him, for He cares for you."

Fear of Man

The fear of man often causes shutdown and social withdrawal. Fear of man usually leaves loving deeds, such as preaching the gospel undone.

REMEDY: Proverbs 29:25 "The fear of man brings a snare, but whoever trusts in the LORD will be safe."

Anxiety

If believers are anxious about natural things, they can get caught up in their souls. Focusing on worry thoughts can make it difficult for believers to allow love to flow from their spirits.

REMEDY: Matthew 6:25–27 "Therefore I say to you, do not worry about your life, what you will eat or what you will drink; nor about your body, what you will put on. Is not life more than food and the body more than clothing? Look at the birds of the air, for they neither sow nor reap nor gather into barns; yet your heavenly Father feeds them. Are you not of more value than they? Which of you by worrying can add one cubit to his stature?"

Trauma

A traumatized heart never functions at its best. Trauma memories can be laden with painful emotions, affecting how a believer thinks and acts.

REMEDY: Psalm 147:3 "He [God] heals the brokenhearted and binds up their wounds."

Rebellion

A rebellious heart is often far from God. Lack of submission to God's will can hinder believers' ability to walk in God's love.

REMEDY: Psalm 107:10–13 "Those who sat in darkness and in the shadow of death, bound in affliction and irons – because they rebelled against the words of God, and despised the counsel of the Most High, therefore He brought down their heart with labor; They fell down, and there was none to help. Then they cried out to the LORD in their trouble, and He saved them out of their distresses."

Abuse

Believers suffering maltreatment and abuse can have mental, emotional, and will problems. Negative thoughts and beliefs and damaged emotions can make it hard for someone's heart to release love. Also, the devil may try to provoke a wounded believer into unloving behavior.

REMEDY: Psalm 34:18 "The Lord is near to those who have a broken heart, and saves such as have a contrite spirit."

Doubt/unbelief

Unbelief is a dangerous mindset. Doubt and unbelief can tie up faith and love, making them inactive.

REMEDY: Hebrews 11:6 "But Without faith it is impossible to please Him, for he who comes to God must believe that He is, and that He is a rewarder of those who diligently seek Him."

The Snare of the Fowler

A fowler is someone who hunts fowl such as ducks and quail. A snare is a trap that is baited with food. A fowler's snare is how hunters catch birds when they stop to take the bait. We know the devil sets up traps for believers. One common trap of the devil is lies (John 8:44). The devil wants believers to think about what is not true so that he (rather than love) can reign over them.

REMEDY: John 8:36 "Therefore if the Son makes you free, you shall be free indeed."

Offense

Believers sometimes judge and condemn others when they are upset. Rather than appearing loving and kind, offended believers can seem withdrawn and cold.

REMEDY: Luke 6:37 "Judge not, and you shall not be judged. Condemn not, and you shall not be condemned. Forgive, and you will be forgiven."

Pride, Anger, Guilt, and Shame

Pride, anger, guilt, and shame can limit love's flow. When believers are proud, they may be isolated and think some situations are not worth their time. Anger is a potent emotion. When people get angry, they can feel consumed by it. When people suffer guilt or shame, these emotions can be so crippling that they hinder people from reaching their full potential relationally.

REMEDY: James 1:19-20 "So then, my beloved brethren, let every man be swift to hear, slow to speak, slow to wrath; for the wrath of man does not produce the righteousness of God."

Mental and Physical Illness

Any disease or affliction can interfere with a person's love walk. When it comes to severe mental and physical illnesses, a person's ability to give and exchange love may be significantly compromised.

REMEDY: Exodus 15:26 "...If you diligently heed the voice of the LORD your God and do what is right in His sight, give ear to His commandments and keep all His statutes, I will put none of the diseases on you which I have brought on the Egyptians. For I am the LORD who heals you."

Curses

A curse is a supernatural work that brings harm. Curses can hinder believers from walking in love and receiving God's blessings. There are a few types of curses believers need to combat, including generational curses, witchcraft curses, and word curses.

REMEDY: Proverbs 26:2 "Like a flitting sparrow, like a flying swallow, so a curse without a cause shall not alight."

Demonic Assignments

Jesus defeated demons at the cross (Colossians 2:15: "Having disarmed principalities and powers, He made a public spectacle of them, triumphing over them in it"). Demonic assignments sometimes hinder believers' loving actions.

Remedy: Luke 10:19 "Behold I give you the authority to trample on serpents and scorpions, and over all the power of the enemy, and nothing shall by any means hurt you."

Prayer Point: Father, remove whatever may be limiting the flow of love from my heart.

CHAPTER 25 KEY POINTS
Heart Constrictors

- ❖ Heart constrictors restrict believers from pouring love from their heart.
- ❖ When heart constrictors are in present, what is inside a person doesn't easily get on the outside.
- ❖ A healthy heart pours out love. A heart that cannot release love is sometimes constricted.
- ❖ There are many causes of heart constriction.
- ❖ When believers try to carry and handle every problem and care, their hearts can get weighed down.
- ❖ Fear of man often leaves loving deeds, such as preaching the gospel undone.
- ❖ Focusing on worry thoughts can make it difficult for believers to allow love to flow from their spirits.
- ❖ Trauma memories can be laden with painful emotions, affecting how a believer thinks and acts.
- ❖ Negative thoughts and beliefs, damaged emotions, and disorders of will can make it hard for someone's heart to release love.
- ❖ Doubt and unbelief can tie up faith and love, making them inactive.
- ❖ The devil wants believers to think about what is not true so that he (rather than love) can reign over them.
- ❖ Rather than appearing loving and kind, offended believers can seem withdrawn and cold.
- ❖ When it comes to severe mental and physical illnesses, a person's ability to give and exchange love may be significantly compromised.
- ❖ Curses can hinder believers from walking in love and receiving God's blessings.
- ❖ Demonic assignments sometimes hinder believers' love walk.

CHAPTER 25 STUDY QUESTIONS
Heart Constrictors

---

1. What is a heart constrictor?

   _____
   _____
   _____
   _____

2. Describe how fear of man may cause heart constriction.

   _____
   _____
   _____
   _____

3. How can rebellion interfere with a believer's love walk?

   _____
   _____
   _____
   _____

4. Why is it hard for someone who was abused to be loving at times?

   _____
   _____
   _____
   _____

5. Can offense keep believers from sharing God's love? Yes No

6. Describe how pride, anger, guilt and shame may limit loving behaviors.

7. How could a curse adversely affect a believer?

Heart Condition Screener

*It is the glory of God to conceal a matter,
But the glory of kings is to search out a matter.*
—Proverbs 25:2

This assessment is based upon material in Part 3 (Heart Conditions). Read each item thoughtfully. Check a statement if it seems generally true about you in the past two weeks. Please view this screener as a brief inventory of the heart. It is not intended to be a definitive tool. Other factors, such as medical problems or temporary life situations, can explain your responses. After completing these questions, you will be more aware of conditions you may be experiencing in your heart.

Heartcry
_____I am facing very stressful life situations.
_____My situation is almost desperate.
_____I feel myself crying out from the depths of my being for help.
_____I feel at the end of myself and my efforts.
_____I am praying a lot more.

Heartsickness
_____I feel like I am losing hope for some things to come.
_____There are things in my life that seem delayed or drawn out.
_____I feel weak, ill, and unwell.
_____I feel like I have a lack of zest for life.
_____I feel low energy.

_____I keep focusing on what I don't have.

Heart Failure
_____My ability to manage my mind, emotions, and will seems to be breaking down.
_____I am feeling overwhelming fatigue.
_____I am having problems managing stress and exertion.
_____I find myself seeking out support and encouragement often.
_____I feel a bit numb and out of it.
_____Sometimes I feel like I can't go on because I am so burdened.

Heartbreak
_____I have been through trauma and it feels as if my heart broke.
_____I feel like I can't function.
_____I feel lifeless in my mind, will, and emotions.
_____I don't want to pray, read the Bible, or go to church.

Heart Abuse
_____I feel like I berate myself a lot.
_____I struggle with negative thoughts about myself.
_____I put myself down and find fault with what I do often.
_____I hate myself.
_____I have low self–esteem.

Heart Wound
_____I've been through recent trauma.
_____I have been through things that overwhelmed my soul.
_____I can get distraught when traumatic events are discussed.
_____I can react disproportionately to situations.

Deceived Heart
_____I feel like I have been turned in the wrong direction.
_____I feel like I have been believing something that wasn't true.
_____I feel like I don't know what's true and what's not true, at times.
_____Sometimes I think I have an exaggerated view of myself.
_____I hear the Word of God but don't do it.

Heart Bound
_____I have some interests that I just can't let go.
_____I feel like some things I must do.
_____I feel constrained by my "musts."
_____I have trouble letting go of people, places, and things.
_____I feel driven to possess money.
_____I feel motivated to seek the easy way or comfort.

Double Heart
_____I feel like I have two conflicting opinions I can't resolve.
_____I may say one thing, but I think differently in my heart.
_____I may say things to people that I don't mean.
_____I feel at war in my thoughts.
_____Sometimes I believe God's Word, and sometimes I don't.
_____I like to participate in the world's way of doing things and God's way.

Hard Heart
_____My heart feels bitter, pitiless, or unfeeling at times.
_____My heart feels dull and insensitive.
_____My heart feels closed off.
_____There are things I think I should do, but I don't want to because I'm upset.
_____I feel angry at others and God, at times.

Fearful Heart
_____I feel like someone or something is a danger or threat to me.
_____Some situations always cause me to feel at risk of harm.
_____I have trouble with my faith because I am full of fear.
_____I avoid evangelizing because of fear, worry, or anxiety.
_____Sometimes I feel like problems are too big for God.
_____I fear people and what they think.

Heart Block
_____I try to act a certain way and find I can't do it.
_____Sometimes, I mean to do something, and then I do the opposite.
_____I feel like things are getting in the way of me following God.

_____I struggle with offense.
_____Sometimes, when I am afraid, I don't do what I ought to do.
_____I suffer from thinking I have to do everything by myself.
_____Sometimes, I feel far from God due to an entrenched sin problem.
_____I don't dream.

Mindbending
_____I have seen and heard things that radically affected how I thought/felt/acted.
_____I have done things I would have never done after I saw or heard something.
_____I have hung around certain people and started acting like them.
_____I have adopted beliefs that I would not normally accept.
_____I have been through trauma and feel that my thinking was radically affected.

Heartworm
_____I find that I hold certain mindsets that hurt rather than help me.
_____I lose friendships because I allow offense to eat away at the relationship.
_____I allow things to take away my trust and confidence in the Lord.
_____I have noticed little things in my life leading to big problems later.

Cancer of the Mind
_____I feel like my mind is overrun with thoughts that I cannot control.
_____I try to think correctly but have trouble doing so.
_____I have a lot of thoughts that seem abnormal.
_____I have ideas that don't line up with my identity or life situation.
_____I feel like I have so many negative thoughts and so few positive thoughts.
_____Sometimes I feel like my mind is oppressed.

Cancer of the Heart
_____Sometimes I feel like evil spirits oppress me.
_____I have trouble hearing from God.
_____Sometimes I act or speak in ways that I am surprised by.

Heart Constrictors

_____I feel like things limit me from walking in love.
_____I have trouble pouring love out of my heart.
_____I feel so burdened by problems that I forget to help others.
_____I suffer anxiety and fear being judged.
_____I had trauma and abuse and have trouble giving and receiving love.
_____I often don't feel well and feel unable to help others.

PART 4

Heart Healing

CHAPTER 26

Christ's Work in Heart Healing

The heart is deceitful above all things, and desperately wicked;
Who can know it?
–Jeremiah 17:9

The Conscious, Preconscious, and Unconscious Mind.

The soul comprises the conscious, preconscious, and unconscious mind, emotions, and will. It is vast! Jeremiah 17:9 says, "The heart is deceitful above all things, and desperately wicked; Who can know it?" People can never fully perceive the soul's countless nuances. Yet, it is wise to learn about its different aspects.

With the conscious mind, people interact with the world through the eyes, ears, nose, mouth, and skin. I can feel the keys under my fingers as I type right now. I see my cat peacefully sleeping beside me, and I smell the lotion I put on my hands and feet. The conscious mind is active and alert and focuses on goals and plans. It's like a processor taking in and organizing sensory data. A lot of what we do each day involves the conscious mind.

The preconscious is material just below the conscious mind's surface. Preconscious material is not the focus of attention. However, it contains things people can readily get in touch with – e.g., beliefs, self–image, fears, and habits. The preconscious influences behavior, but sometimes outside immediate awareness.

The unconscious mind contains material that is outside awareness. The unconscious mind plays a significant role in thinking, reacting, and acting. Unlike material in the conscious and preconscious mind, beliefs, thoughts, feelings, and memories in the unconscious can be difficult to access. As a psychologist, this type of material is often what I am helping patients to uncover and understand. Some examples of material in the unconscious mind may include traumatic memories, shame, guilt, anger, and secrets.

One way material gets into the unconscious mind is by repression. Repression is the soul's automatic way of dealing with overwhelming or threatening material. Repression is protective. It puts things under to minimize disturbance to the soul. I liken material being pushed outside awareness (almost like it is behind a wall) to what someone might do to an animal that bites. You contain it. Repression seems like a gift from God. It's a built-in mechanism to help people not succumb to overwhelming circumstances. However, when memories are buried without being fully processed, they can cause problems.

Heart Memory.

The heart has a great capacity to form and retain memories. It's a fascinating timepiece. Like the rings in a tree trunk, life events, and inner experiences are logged within the heart; memories in the heart can sometimes last a lifetime when the initial impression is strong. No one would remember what they had for breakfast seven weeks ago. Almost everyone would recall winning a car or sustaining significant injuries in a boating accident. While memories can be a blessing, when they are traumatic, they can cause harm. Trauma memories can be like a landmine. Untouched, they can lie dormant and seemingly innocuous. Just graze a trauma memory, and a person may explode with painful thoughts, feelings, and even physical symptoms. Unprocessed (or not fully processed) trauma memories differ from everyday memories. Trauma memories are not lifeless. They contain energies that are at times pent up.

I worked with a patient once who had resolved his acute issues and became psychologically stable. Then, unexpectedly, the person came to the session one day in overwhelming emotional turmoil. The person said he had returned from a retreat with people who repeatedly acted cold and withdrawn. He said people were in cliques, and no one invited him to join. He was left feeling alone in the midst of many. This person had been severely neglected and rejected as a child—exposure to similar conditions tapped into parts of his heart that were still wounded. The result was intense emotional pain seemingly out of the blue. We started processing the trauma. He allowed buried material to surface, and the man recalled specific traumatic childhood events, including having family barely talk to him, family forgetting to pick him up from events, feeling ignored by a football coach, and repeatedly being given the cold shoulder from peers in his friend group for having different opinions. Processing helped bring some relief, comfort, and insights.

Uncovering the Unconscious Work of Christ.

People can suffer significant issues including but not limited to depression, anxiety, delusions, psychosis, rage, low self-esteem, and self-hatred, and may not know why. There are 86,400 seconds in a day and over 900 million seconds in 30 years. That's a lot of time for things to happen to the soul. No Ph.D., M.D., or LCSW can figure out the soul, let alone the wounding that can occur.

When dealing with trauma-related soul issues, people can be helped by talking through them. However, people can reap more benefits when they bring their soul problems to God. He made the soul. He is the only one who knows where it is and how to fix it. Psalm 23:3 says, "He restores my soul…" It doesn't say, believers make their souls new again. God is the expert at soul restoration. People can often manage material in the conscious and preconscious mind. These are things that are readily known and noticed. What can be difficult and sometimes impossible to deal with are soul issues that are not understood or outside awareness.

How many of the heart conditions outlined in Part 3 of this book did you fully understand? How many were you aware of? Heart conditions can be subtle. They can be operating under the radar. Once identified, they can be challenging to treat. Finding root causes can be like looking for a needle in a haystack. No matter a believer's heart condition, God can heal them all. Matthew 12:15 says, "But when Jesus knew it, He withdrew from there. And great multitudes followed Him, and He healed them all." Not some. All.

God can help believers needing soul healing by identifying problematic material in the unconscious mind, revealing the primary causes of problems, and restoring the soul's functioning. Imagine a believer suffering overwhelming anxiety and tension headaches but not knowing why. A good prayer might be, "Father, I have anxiety and headaches. I have no idea why. Please reveal the root causes and bring healing." God may reveal that the believer has repressed anger related to previous trauma. As the believer processes past trauma and learns new ways of managing anger, that person may have less anxiety and fewer headaches.

God tells us in Matthew 7:7, "Ask, and it will be given to you; seek, and you will find; knock, and it will be opened to you." James 1:5 says, "If any of you lacks wisdom, let him ask of God, who gives to all liberally and without reproach, and it will be given to him." When believers ask, they receive. There is no reason for not knowing why something is happening. God always reveals to heal. Believers do well to press in. God has all the answers. He wants believers healed and set free.

Sometimes, believers don't need to pray about an issue. God may suddenly start shedding light on it. For example, a man may start noticing how rageful he gets when ignored in social situations. The Holy Spirit may highlight the issue so God can bring healing. The root of the problem may be the trauma of never being listened to or taken seriously as a child. Consider a believer who starts feeling down about chronic prayerlessness. While this wasn't an issue, the believer doesn't feel good about never praying. God may want to bring light and healing. This person may have had parents who never prayed. Independence rather than dependence was encouraged. Once the roots of the prayerlessness are revealed, healing can come. Imagine a woman getting sick a lot but never knowing why. God may spontaneously bring to her remembrance her visits to psychics during college. She may realize God is highlighting a possible reason for her illness issue. When the reason for something is concealed, God can reveal it.

Consider Barry. He had a lot going for himself. However, his relationship with his father was terrible. Whenever Barry got around his father, he would disconnect and shut down. He would try to listen and ask questions but found himself falling back into old patterns of remaining aloof and uninvolved. This led to Barry feeling guilty. Barry said he had forgiven his father for big arguments in the past and was trying to be active in his family life. But the problems continued. I suspected that Barry had soul wounds outside of his conscious awareness. After we prayed about it, Barry started remembering important childhood details. Barry remembered that his father was often in an angry and irritable mood. He never smiled and seemed to be in a different world. Barry remembered happily approaching his dad, only to walk away sad. His father barely communicated with him. And when he did, it was often to criticize, complain, or express frustration with Barry. We realized Barry suffered verbal and emotional mistreatment, and all those hurts were buried in his unconscious. Fear. Doubt. Insecurity. Performance orientation. Perfectionism. Abandonment. Offense. Bitterness. Anger. These were all unconsciously affecting Barry. Prayer brought God into Barry's situation, and hidden things were revealed. With insights and healing from God, Barry's soul and family relationships finally started improving. Barry felt more peaceful, happy, and free from guilt. He only wished he had started praying about his issue sooner.

Soul problems don't have to be faced alone. Self-help books and counseling provide valuable information and guidance but can fall short. Call on God. Watch Him reveal and heal acute and chronic conditions, once hidden and unknown.

Prayer Point: Father, please reveal and heal problematic material in my unconscious mind and restore my soul to full functioning.

CHAPTER 26 KEY POINTS
Christ's Work in Heart Healing

- ❖ The soul is comprised of the conscious, preconscious, and unconscious mind, emotions, and will. It is vast!
- ❖ Jeremiah 17:9 says, "The heart is deceitful above all things, and desperately wicked; Who can know it?"
- ❖ Unlike material in the conscious and preconscious mind, beliefs, thoughts, feelings, and memories in the unconscious can be difficult to access.
- ❖ Some examples of material in the unconscious mind may include traumatic memories, shame, guilt, anger, and secrets.
- ❖ One way material gets into the unconscious mind is by repression.
- ❖ Repression is the soul's automatic way of dealing with material that is overwhelming or too threatening.
- ❖ When memories are buried without being fully processed, they can cause problems.
- ❖ Memories in the heart can sometimes last a lifetime when the initial impression is strong.
- ❖ Trauma memories can be like a landmine.
- ❖ People can suffer significant issues including but not limited to depression, anxiety, delusions, psychosis, rage, low self-esteem, and self-hatred, and may not know why.
- ❖ There are 86,400 seconds in a day, and over 900 million seconds in 30 years. That's a lot of time for things to happen to the soul.
- ❖ When dealing with soul issues, people are helped by talking through them.
- ❖ People can reap more benefits when they bring their soul problems to God.
- ❖ God made the soul. He is the only one who knows where it is and how to fix it.
- ❖ What can be difficult and sometimes impossible to deal with are soul issues that are not understood or outside awareness.

- ❖ God can help believers needing soul healing by identifying problematic material in the unconscious mind, revealing the primary causes of problems, and restoring the soul's functioning.
- ❖ God always reveals to heal. Believers do well to press in. God has all the answers. He wants believers healed and set free.
- ❖ Soul problems don't have to be faced alone.
- ❖ Self–help books and counseling provide valuable information and guidance but can fall short.
- ❖ Call on God. Watch Him reveal and heal acute and chronic conditions, once hidden and unknown.

CHAPTER 26 STUDY QUESTIONS
Christ's Work in Heart Healing

---

1. Describe the conscious, preconscious, and unconscious mind.

2. Write out Jeremiah 17:9. What does it say about the heart?

3. What kind of memories tend to be enduring?

4. Describe how trauma memories can be like a landmine.

_____
_____
_____
_____

5. Name three ways God can help believers with issues that have no known cause.

_____
_____
_____
_____

6. Name one unresolved soul problem you have and ask God for help with it.

_____
_____
_____
_____

27
CHAPTER

Fostering Heart Health

*Who may ascend into the hill of the Lord? Or
who may stand in His holy place?
He who has clean hands and a pure heart, who
has not lifted up his soul to an idol.*
—Psalm 24:3–4

If left alone, most things tend toward disorder rather than order. Just neglect your kitchen counter or laundry for a while. Things get cluttered, disorganized, and dirty. The same is true with the heart. Without regular care, the heart can start to flounder rather than flourish.

In Genesis 2:15, Adam was put in the garden to "...tend and keep it." Believers must do the same with their hearts. Having an outstanding outlook, a faith–filled confession, or a positive mindset doesn't come automatically. Strategies to foster heart health are outlined in this chapter. Review these practices regularly until they become routine. Scriptures are like medicine to the soul, so don't forget to also meditate on the Word of God. Over time, you should see improvements in your heart health.

<u>Praise</u>. Praise is a powerful weapon against sadness and feelings of defeat. At Jericho, praise preceded the victory.

FOSTERING HEART HEALTH

> Psalm 9:1 "I will praise You, O LORD, with my whole heart; I will tell of all your marvelous works."

<u>Strive to have the right heart attitude</u>. A bad attitude can ruin a believer's day. Look to the Lord for help in thinking and believing for good things.

> First Thessalonians 5:16–18 "Rejoice always, pray without ceasing, in everything give thanks; for this is the will of God in Christ Jesus for you."

<u>Ask God to search your heart</u>. Most believers have a limited understanding of what is going on in their hearts. Asking God to look for problems in the heart is an excellent heart health strategy.

> Psalm 139:23–24 "Search me, O God, and know my heart; try me and know my anxieties; and see if there is any wicked way in me, and lead me in the way everlasting."

<u>Pour out your heart to the Lord</u>. Talking is an excellent tool for revealing what is in the heart. It also feels good when believers "get something off their chest."

> Psalm 142:1–3 "I cry out to the LORD with my voice; with my voice to the LORD I make my supplication. I pour out my complaints before Him; I declare before Him my trouble. When my spirit was overwhelmed within me, then You knew my path. In the way in which I walk they have secretly set a snare for me."

<u>Seek the Lord</u>. Life is hard. Believers must learn to go to the Lord for help and support regularly.

> Psalm 34:4–6 "I sought the LORD, and He heard me, and delivered me from all my fears. They looked to Him and were radiant, and their faces were not ashamed. This

poor man cried out, and the LORD heard him, and saved him out of all his troubles."

Know the Truth. God's Word has been given to believers to help them address the issues of life. Regularly read the Bible to receive support, understanding, and wisdom.

> John 8:31–32 "Then Jesus said to those Jews who believed Him, 'If you abide in My word, you are My disciples indeed. And you shall know the truth, and the truth shall make you free.'"

Meditate within your Heart. Pondering the Word of God in the heart is an excellent way to keep the mind from overfocusing on problems and painful emotions.

> Psalm 4:4 "Be angry, and do not sin. Meditate within your heart on your bed and be still."

Get Understanding. When believers don't understand something, this can set up conditions for problems and failure. Gaining comprehension and insight is essential for heart health.

> Proverbs 4:7 "Wisdom is the principal thing; therefore get wisdom. And in all your getting, get understanding."

Know that the Lord hears you. In the world, believers can feel unheard and ignored. Knowing God listens and cares about what believers are going through can promote peace of mind.

> Psalm 34:17 "The righteous cry out, and the LORD hears, and delivers them out of all their troubles.

Pray and enjoy Peace. Praying about concerns helps believers release and relax. Don't neglect this most important way of fostering a peaceful heart.

> Philippians 4:6–7 "Be anxious for nothing, but in everything by prayer and supplication, with thanksgiving, let your requests be made known to God; and the peace of God, which surpasses all understanding, will guard your hearts and minds through Christ Jesus."

<u>Return to God</u>. Believers sometimes drift from God. Don't condemn yourself. Don't be afraid. God is not mad. Run to Him and ask Him for help to start walking with Him again.

> Joel 2:13 "So rend your heart, and not your garments; Return to the LORD your God, for He is gracious and merciful, slow to anger, and of great kindness; and He relents from doing harm."

<u>Speak to your soul</u>. Cheerleading the soul is a good idea. When the soul starts to struggle, it is a good idea to encourage the soul to minimize angst and upset.

> Psalm 42:5 "Why are you cast down, O my soul? And why are you disquieted within me? Hope in God, for I shall yet praise Him for the help of his countenance."

<u>Resist an intellectual spirit</u>. It is tempting to try to figure everything out. But spiritual things must be revealed by God. Believers need to ensure they trust God and not their interpretation of things.

> Proverbs 3:5–6 "Trust in the LORD with all your heart, and lean not on your own understanding; In all your ways acknowledge Him, and He shall direct your paths."

<u>Let not your Heart be troubled</u>. God Himself told believers not to allow their hearts to be overwhelmed. Believers must manage their hearts and put out any fires that start there.

> John 14:27 "Peace I leave with you, My peace I give to you; not as the world gives do I give to you. Let not your heart be troubled, neither let it be afraid."

<u>Draw strength from other believers</u>. After salvation, believers are put into the body of Christ. There is a rich inheritance in the body. What one believer lacks, another may be able to supply. Don't forget to turn to other believers for support during difficult times.

> Ephesians 1:18 "The eyes of your understanding being enlightened; that you may know what is the hope of His calling, what are the riches of the glory of His inheritance in the saints."

<u>Minimize perfectionism</u>. Believers must learn to strive for excellence and not perfection. God doesn't expect perfection. He wants us to trust and believe in what Jesus did in fulfilling all the law requirements. Minimizing perfectionism can promote peace in believers' hearts.

> Second Corinthians 5:21 "For He made Him who knew no sin to be sin for us, that we might become the righteousness of God in Him."

Prayer Point: Father, help me to put into practice strategies that will promote the health of my heart.

CHAPTER 27 KEY POINTS
Fostering Heart Health

- ❖ Without regular care, the heart can start to flounder rather than flourish.
- ❖ In Genesis 2:15, Adam was put in the garden to "...tend and keep it."
- ❖ Having an outstanding outlook, a faith–filled confession, or a positive mindset doesn't come automatically.
- ❖ Scriptures are like medicine to the soul, so don't forget to also meditate on the Word.
- ❖ Praising, having the right heart attitude, asking God to search your heart, and pouring out your heart to the Lord are excellent heart health strategies.
- ❖ Seeking the Lord, praying, returning to God, speaking to the soul, resisting an intellectual spirit, and drawing strength from other believers can help promote heart health.
- ❖ Minimizing perfectionism can promote peace in believers' hearts.

CHAPTER 27 STUDY QUESTIONS
Fostering Heart Health

1. What does it mean to foster heart health?

   _____
   _____
   _____
   _____

2. What do you currently do to foster your heart's health?

   _____
   _____
   _____
   _____

3. Scripture meditation is like _____ to the soul.

4. Will regular review and confession of the Word of God foster heart health? Yes No

5. List 3 strategies for fostering heart health.

   _____
   _____
   _____
   _____

6. How might believers incorporate heart health strategies into their daily routine?

CHAPTER 28

Contrite Heart

*The sacrifices of God are a broken spirit, a broken and a contrite heart –
these O God You will not despise.*
–Psalm 51:17

It's not easy to admit wrongdoing, but it is a beautiful act in God's eyes. That's because sin separates believers from God. Isaiah 59:2 says, "But your iniquities have separated you from your God; and your sins have hidden his face from you, so that He will not hear." God desires believers to have a contrite heart. Having a contrite heart is about being profoundly penitent and repentant. It is a heart posture of unreservedly and openly confessing wrongdoing while seeking God for forgiveness, healing, and relationship restoration.

Having a contrite heart is not knowing you did wrong intellectually. Anyone can make a list of sin problems. If believers don't feel deeply convicted, they can say "I'm sorry" all they want – but it won't do much. When believers are contrite, they feel sorrowful and humbled, having done wrong. If there is ever a situation when God's ears perk up, it's when believers have a contrite heart. God listens to people who are deeply sorry. He listens to them and doesn't disregard their prayers. While it doesn't feel great, having a contrite heart is a good thing. When believers realize they are doing wrong and have come to the end of their way, God can rush in with mercy, grace, and truth.

Consider David. In his weakness, he plotted murder and slept with another man's wife. Psalm 51 is believed to be his tender prayer for mercy and forgiveness. It's an excellent picture of a contrite heart. When believers are contrite, they don't try to defend themselves. They are transparent. There are "no skeletons in the closet." No secret sources of shame or hidden sin. God forgave David. He even sent a prophet to give him the message of mercy and grace. Psalm 51:1–4 says,

> Have mercy on me, O God, according to Your lovingkindness; according to the multitude of Your tender mercies, blot out my transgressions. Wash me thoroughly from my iniquity, and cleanse me from my sin. For I acknowledge my transgressions, and my sin is always before me. Against You, You only, have I sinned, and done this evil in Your sight–That You may be found just when You speak, and blameless when you judge.

Having a contrite heart acknowledges sin for what it is–egregious in the sight of God.

One hindrance to receiving the benefits of a contrite heart is condemnation. This is of Satan's kingdom. It is not of God. The devil clothes condemnation in feeling bad for a wrong that was done. Along with feeling bad can come sadness, self-hate, and self-denigration. A sense of having done wrong when believers sin is normal. But Jesus died for all sins, so believers must be determined to receive the gift of righteousness (Romans 5:17: "For if by the one man's offense death reigned through the one, much more those who receive abundance of grace and of the gift of righteousness will reign in life through the One, Jesus Christ"). Believers are righteous in Christ; they just need to appropriate that truth.

Instead of thinking, "I've made so many mistakes," believers benefit from thinking, "My mistakes are part of my story for God's glory." Instead of, "I should have known better," believers must think, "I was not born spiritually mature. As God's child, I must grow into all God has called me to be." Instead of the thought, "This sin is too bad for God to forgive," believers must think, "If Moses killed a person and God went on to use him mightily, I'm good." Believers must realize that God is merciful and forgiving no matter how bad the sin might be. So, break your heart and thank God for the forgiveness and cleansing He can provide.

Prayer Point: Father, please give me a contrite heart and help me to come to You when I am struggling with sin.

CHAPTER 28 KEY POINTS
Contrite Heart

- ❖ Psalm 51:17 "The sacrifices of God are a broken spirit, a broken and a contrite heart – these O God You will not despise."
- ❖ It's not easy to admit wrongdoing, but it is a beautiful act in God's eyes.
- ❖ God desires believers to have a contrite heart.
- ❖ Having a contrite heart is about being deeply penitent and repentant. It is a heart posture of unreservedly and openly confessing wrongdoing while seeking God for forgiveness, healing, and relationship restoration.
- ❖ Having a contrite heart is not knowing you did wrong intellectually.
- ❖ When believers are contrite, they feel sorrowful and humbled in their heart having done wrong.
- ❖ If there is ever a situation when God's ears perk up, its when believers have a contrite heart.
- ❖ When believers realize they are doing wrong and have come to the end of their way, God can rush in with mercy, grace, and truth.
- ❖ When believers are contrite, they don't try to defend themselves. They are transparent. There are no "skeletons in the closet." No secret sources of shame or hidden sin.
- ❖ One hindrance to receiving the benefits of a contrite heart is condemnation.
- ❖ The devil clothes condemnation in feeling bad for the wrong that was done.
- ❖ Believers are righteous in Christ; they just need to appropriate that truth.
- ❖ Believers must realize that God is merciful and forgiving no matter how bad the sin might be.

CHAPTER 28 STUDY QUESTIONS
Contrite Heart

1. What is a contrite heart?

2. Name two qualities of a contrite heart.

3. What is God's response to a contrite heart?

4. Was David contrite when he confessed his sin of murder and adultery?

5. Write out Psalm 51:1–2. What parts stand out to you?

6. What can hinder the benefits of a contrite heart?

7. Search your heart for any condemning thoughts. How can you eliminate them?

29
CHAPTER

Healthy Heartcries

And this is eternal life, that they may know You, the only true God, and Jesus Christ whom You have sent.
–John 17:3

While there are heartcries that signal trouble, there are also heartcries that are good. Healthy heartcries are passionate, heartfelt sentiments directed to God. They are not birthed from calamity but an earnest desire for something righteous and just. Both new and mature believers can have healthy heartcries. Healthy heartcries can be a sign of a vibrant inner life. The absence of healthy heartcries might suggest complacency or lukewarmness.

Below is a list of healthy heartcries. If you have never had passionate prayers for growth, this list may help jump–start your prayer life.

Say: Lord, I cry to You:

> ...to know You more.
> ...for spiritual revelation.
> ...to know what You are calling me to do.
> ...to know Your general will.
> ...to know Your specific will for my life.
> ...for justice.
> ...for wisdom and understanding.
> ...for protection.
> ...for guidance.
> ...for support and strength.
> ...for connection.
> ...to know more about heaven.
> ...to understand Your mysteries.
> ...to see Your glory.

Lord, I cry to You:

> ...to make me more like You.
> ...to help me worship You in spirit and truth.
> ...to direct my steps.
> ...to move in my situation(s) for good.
> ...for enlightenment.
> ...to give me ears to hear and eyes to see.
> ...for help to walk in the Spirit.
> ...for help to speak Your language.
> ...for help decreeing and declaring Your Word.
> ...for help making a joyful noise to You.
> ...for help to walk with You daily.
> ...for help to prophesy.
> ...for provision to come from every direction.
> ...for help to move in the spiritual gifts as the Holy Spirit wills.
> ...for help to slay giants like David did.
> ...to make me humble, patient, and peaceful.
> ...for help to take territory daily.
> ...for help to be a soul winner.

...to be a bride of Christ and not just a believer.
...to pour out the blessing of Abraham in my life.
...for help to speak as You do (with creative power).
...for help to speak with commanding authority.

Lord, I cry to You:

...for help to see You as Creator but also as Father and friend.
...for sanctified relationships.
...to hear from You in dreams.
...for help to envision Your kind of blessings.
...for Your solutions.
...for help to dance as David danced.
...for help in doing great exploits.
...for help to always lend and never borrow.
...for help to reign with Christ.
...to bear much fruit (100 fold).
...to quickly discern and defeat demonic attacks.
...to see myself through Your eyes.
...for help to realize my value for the kingdom of God.
...to discern Your direction in all situations.
...for Your timing.
...for help in waiting on You.
...to help tear down walls.
...for an ongoing harvest.
...for prosperity in every area of life.
...to save all people.
...to bless and protect all people.

Prayer Point: Father, I know You hear the cries of my heart. Help me to draw near to You and ask for my heart's desires.

CHAPTER 29 KEY POINTS
Healthy Heartcries

- ❖ While there are heartcries that signal trouble, there are also heartcries that are good.
- ❖ Healthy heartcries are passionate, heartfelt sentiments directed to God.
- ❖ Healthy heartcries are not birthed from calamity, but from a fervent desire for something righteous and just.
- ❖ Both new and mature believers can have healthy heartcries.
- ❖ Healthy heartcries can be a sign of a vibrant inner life.
- ❖ The absence of healthy heartcries might suggest complacency or lukewarmness.

CHAPTER 29 STUDY QUESTIONS
Healthy Heartcries

1. What is a healthy heartcry?

2. Review the list of healthy heartcries. Which ones stood out to you and why?

3. Create three of your own healthy heartcries.

CHAPTER 30

Heart Guards

For as he thinks in his heart, so is he.
—Proverbs 23:7

In the mental health field, positive self–statements or affirmations are encouraged. Affirmations are good and support the soul. Positive self–statements can help reduce negative thinking and give self–esteem a lift. I recommend them to all of my patients, knowing Proverbs 23:7 says, "For as he thinks in his heart, so is he…" What believers think about defines who they are. It sets the boundaries for their inner life.

There is a way to supercharge affirmations. A person can supercharge affirmations by saying something positive based on truth from God's Word. Instead of just saying, "I'm gonna have a good day today," or "I can get through this," a believer could say, "The Lord orders my steps, and He delights in my way" (Psalm 37:23) or "God is for me, who can be against me" (Romans 8:31).

Heart guards are maxims based upon Bible truths that can help protect the heart from lies, fear, doubt, and unbelief. Below are some examples of heart guards. Many verses from the Bible can be turned into heart guard statements. The way to do this is to condense a Bible verse or passage into a few words. Heart guards are an easy and reliable way of encouraging the soul. They take a few seconds, and because God's Word backs them, they are power–packed. Heart guards can bring hope to the soul. However, they should not replace Scripture reading, meditation, and declaration.

1. Heart guard against cares. Declaration: "**God's got this.**"
    First Peter 5:6–7 "Therefore humble yourselves under the mighty hand of God, that He may exalt you in due time, casting all your care upon Him, for He cares for you."

2. Heart guard against pride. Declaration: "**To God be all the glory.**"
    Proverbs 16:18 "Pride goes before destruction, and a haughty spirit before a fall."

3. Heart guard against laboring in vain. Declaration: "**I am fruitful in Christ.**"
    John 15:5 "I am the vine, you are the branches. He who abides in Me, and I in him, bears much fruit; for without Me you can do nothing."

4. Heart guard against sorrow. Declaration: "**Jesus rejoiced and so will I.**"
    Luke 10:21 "In that hour Jesus rejoiced in the Spirit and said, "I thank You, Father, Lord of heaven and earth, that You have hidden these things from the wise and prudent and revealed them to babes. Even so, Father, for so it seemed good in Your sight."

5. Heart guard against sexual sin. Declaration: "**I run from temptation**."
    Genesis 39:11–12 "But it happened about this time, when Joseph went into the house to do his work, and none of the men of the house was inside, that she [Potiphar's wife] caught him by his garment, saying, "Lie with me." But he left his garment in her hand, and fled and ran outside."

6. Heart guard against inner turmoil. Declaration: "**My mind is peaceful.**"
    Isaiah 26:3 "You will keep him in perfect peace, whose mind is stayed on You, because he trusts in You."

7. Heart guard against a sense of defeat. Declaration: "**I always triumph in Christ.**"

    Second Corinthians 2:14 "Now thanks be to God who always leads us in triumph in Christ, and through us diffuses the fragrance of His knowledge in every place."

8. Heart guard against loneliness. Declaration: "**God is always with me.**"

    Deuteronomy 31:6 "Be strong and of good courage, do not fear nor be afraid of them; for the Lord your God, He is the One who goes with you. He will not leave you nor forsake you."

9. 9. Heart guard against hopelessness. Declaration: "**God has a good future for me.**"

    Jeremiah 29:11 "For I know the thoughts that I think toward you, says the Lord, thoughts of peace and not of evil, to give you a future and a hope."

10. Heart guard against faithlessness. Declaration: "**God said it. I believe it.**"

    Matthew 21:21 "So Jesus answered and said to them, "Assuredly, I say to you, if you have faith and do not doubt, you will not only do what was done to the fig tree, but also if you say to this mountain, 'Be removed and be cast into the sea,' it will be done."

11. Heart guard against fatigue. Declaration: "**God sustains me.**"

    Psalm 55:22 "Cast your burden on the LORD and He shall sustain you; He shall never permit the righteous to be moved."

12. Heart guard against low self–esteem. Declaration: "**I am valuable to God.**"

    First Corinthians 1:26–29 "For you see your calling, brethren, that not many wise according to the flesh, not many mighty, not many noble, are called. But God has chosen the foolish things of the world to put to shame the wise, and God has chosen the weak things of the world to put to shame the things which are mighty. And the base things of the world and the things which are despised God has chosen, and the things which are not, to bring to nothing the things that are, that no flesh should glory in His presence."

13. Heart guard against self-effort. Declaration: "**God empowers me.**"
    Ephesians 6:10 "Finally, my brethren, be strong in the Lord and in the power of His might."

Prayer Point: Father, help me to guard my heart by speaking Your truth often.

CHAPTER 30 KEY POINTS
Heart Guards

- ❖ Positive self–statements or affirmations can help reduce negative thinking and give self–esteem a lift.
- ❖ Proverbs 23:7 says, "For as he thinks in his heart, so is he…"
- ❖ What believers think about defines who they are. It sets the boundaries for their inner life.
- ❖ A person can supercharge affirmations by saying something positive based on truth from God's Word.
- ❖ Heart guards are maxims based upon Bible truths that can help protect the heart from lies, fear, doubt, and unbelief.
- ❖ Many verses from the Bible can be turned into heart guard statements.
- ❖ Heart guards are an easy and reliable way of encouraging the soul.
- ❖ Heart guards can bring hope to the soul.
- ❖ Heart guards should not replace Scripture reading, meditation, and declaration.
- ❖ Sample heart guards: "God's got this." "To God be all the glory." "I am fruitful in Christ." "Jesus rejoiced in spirit and so will I." "I run from temptation." "My mind is peaceful." "I always triumph in Christ." "God is always with me." "God has a good future for me." "God said it. I believe it." "God sustains me." "I am valuable to God." "God empowers me."

CHAPTER 30 STUDY QUESTIONS
Heart Guards

1. What is a heart guard?

2. Write out Proverbs 23:7 and explain what it means.

3. How does a believer create a heart guard?

4. Read the list of heard guards in this chapter and write out three of your favorites.

5. What are two of your favorite Bible verses?

_____

_____

_____

_____

6. Create one heart guard from a Bible verse.

_____

_____

_____

_____

Chapter 31

Qualities of a Healthy Heart

I will praise You, O LORD, with my whole heart;
I will tell of all your marvelous works.
—Psalm 9:1

Various heart conditions were introduced in Part 3, some mild and others catastrophic in their effects on a person's soul and life. In this chapter, the contents of a healthy heart will be reviewed.

Order

A healthy heart will have order and structure. The contents will not be a jumbled mess like a box of jigsaw puzzle pieces. A believer's heart will have form like a tree with roots, trunk, branches, and leaves. Believers are called "trees" in the Bible. Isaiah 61:3 says, "…That they may be called trees of righteousness, the planting of the LORD that He may be glorified." Trees grow systematically. First, the seed in the soil, the roots, stem, and leaves, and then repeated cycles of growth and rest. The development of a tree is orderly and progressive. Trees continue to grow unless winds and storms severely damage them. Like trees, healthy hearts go through stages and cycles of growth and can also be damaged.

God likes to dwell in an orderly place. Consider the orderliness of the places of worship in the Old Testament. In Exodus 26, the description of the mobile tabernacle is exact. There were expectations about the layout, who could be there, what they do, and who could take it down. When Solomon built the Temple, it was also very organized and with a specific design and contents. There was no clutter or mess.

When a person's heart is out of order, certain beliefs, thoughts, imaginations, emotions, and behaviors may not fit a person's age, intellectual capacity, educational achievement, or level of spiritual development. Psychological arrested development happens when trauma has impaired a person's development of emotional maturity. Rather than mature emotional responses to stresses, a person with arrested development may demonstrate behaviors typical in children (e.g., tantrums, crying, yelling, freezing, and hiding). Due to trauma, a person's inner and outer life can be out of order.

Wholeness

Healthy hearts are "whole." Integrated. They are not splintered and broken. Some people do not have whole hearts. Some life events can "subtract" from a person's heart. For example, I've met people who have suffered trauma and have no positive emotions. They only experience sadness, anxiety, fear, anger, or other negative emotions. I've met people who have trouble using logic in problem–solving. It's like they are all emotion and no reason. I've met others who can't remember small or vast parts of their past. They have very poor memories. Some people easily dissociate and sometimes can't even remember important life events such as their graduation or wedding day.

Positive Expectation

A healthy heart is full of positive expectation. When believers walk by faith and not sight, they anticipate the good God will do (2nd Corinthians 5:7). Hebrews 11:1 says, "Now faith is the substance of things hoped for, the evidence of things not seen. Faith says, "I've got this spiritually and am expecting it at any moment in the natural." If God's Word said it, He will do it (Romans 4:20–22: "He did not waiver at the promise of God through unbelief, but was strengthened in faith, giving glory to God, and being fully convinced that what He had promised He was also able to perform. And therefore 'it was accounted to him for righteousness'").

Love

Romans 5:5 says, "Now hope does not disappoint, because the love of God has been poured out in our hearts by the Holy Spirit who was given to us." Love is a wonderful gift from God. All believers have a deposit of love in their hearts. Love empowers believers' behavior. Compared to love, all other things seem insignificant (1 Corinthians 13:2–3: "And though I have the gift of prophecy, and understand all mysteries and all knowledge, and though I have all faith, so that I could remove mountains, but have not love, I am nothing. And though I bestow all my goods to feed the poor, and though I give my body to be burned, but have not love, it profits me nothing"). No doubt, the most significant thing to possess is love.

Peace

A healthy heart is full of peace. Like love, God has given believers peace. John 14:27 says, "Peace I leave with you, My peace I give to you; not as the world gives do I give to you. Let not your heart be troubled, neither let it be afraid." Jesus said he has given believers peace. Like love, experiencing peace may not be automatic. Believers can get caught up with the chaos and stress of the world and may think anxious thoughts. Believers must choose to let peace be present in the soul. Colossians 3:15 says, "And let the peace of God rule in your hearts, to which also you were called in one body; and be thankful." Peace cannot reign unless believers let it. The things of this world and the mind must be subdued so that the peace God deposited deep within can come forth.

Joy

A healthy heart contains joy. Romans 15:13 says, "Now may the God of hope fill you with all joy and peace in believing, that you may abound in hope by the power of the Holy Spirit." Like love and peace, God can fill believers with joy. Being a part of God's family is about being joyful. Romans 14:17 says, "For the kingdom of God is not eating and drinking, but righteousness and peace and joy in the Holy Spirit." Who wouldn't be exuberantly happy knowing the Creator of the whole universe is your Father? The world may say, "Oh, things are so terrible." But believers can truly rejoice always because of their rich inheritance in Christ Jesus (Philippians 4:4: "Rejoice in the Lord always. Again I will say, "rejoice!")

Hope

A healthy heart has hope. When believers know the true nature of God (e.g., He is sovereign, merciful, forgiving, and able to heal, deliver, rescue, and provide), their hearts can fill with hope. By asking according to the Word of God, believers confidently expect to receive help from God. Even though life can get rough, believers can expect good to come. Second Corinthians 4:16-17 says, "Therefore we do not lose heart. Even though our outward man is perishing, yet the inward man is being renewed day by day. For our light affliction, which is but for a moment, is working for us a far more exceeding and eternal weight of glory." When believers persevere in life, God reassures them that glory awaits. That's good news! Hebrews 6:19 says, "This hope we have as an anchor of the soul, both sure and steadfast, and which enters the Presence behind the veil." Hope has a stabilizing force on believers' minds. The assurance of knowing everything will be OK is priceless.

Wisdom

A healthy heart contains God's wisdom. There is earthly wisdom (James 3:15: "This wisdom does not descend from above, but is earthly, sensual, demonic."). Worldly wisdom isn't what believers should seek to possess. Godly wisdom is like gold. Proverbs 4:7 says, "Wisdom is the principal thing; Therefore get wisdom, and in all your getting, get understanding." If God tells believers to get wisdom, we should get some. James 1:5 says, "If any of you lacks wisdom, let him ask of God, who gives to all liberally and without reproach, and it will be given to him." God wants believers to be wise. If believers ask for wisdom, they will receive it. Before the Holy Spirit entered believers' hearts, the Israelites relied on the High Priest for guidance from God (Exodus 28:30). Today, God directly gives believers wisdom in their hearts by the Holy Spirit.

Tenderness

A healthy heart is soft and tender. A person with tenderness can feel the infirmities of others and can also easily say, "I forgive you" or "I'm sorry." In contrast, a hard heart can be full of pride, bitterness, and resentment and may not be able to offer forgiveness to someone. Ephesians 4:32 says, "And be kind to one another, tenderhearted, forgiving one another, even as God in Christ forgave you." You may wonder if you have what it takes to be tenderhearted? The Bible says you do. In Ezekiel 36:36 says, "I will give you a new heart and put a new spirit within you; I will take the heart of stone out of your flesh and give you a heart of flesh." A heart of stone is unfeeling. Rigid. I heart of flesh can be moved. It is soft. A heart of flesh has been transformed by the Lord. It is not longer difficult, unmovable, or rebellious.

Prayer Point: Father, please create in me a beautiful heart with order, wholeness, positive expectation, love, peace, joy, hope, wisdom, and tenderness.

CHAPTER 31 KEY POINTS
Qualities of a Healthy Heart

- ❖ A healthy heart will have order and structure.
- ❖ Like a tree with roots, trunk, branches, and leaves, a believer's heart will have form.
- ❖ When a person's heart is out of order, certain beliefs, thoughts, imaginations, emotions, and behaviors, may not fit a person's age, intellectual capacity, education level, and skill sets.
- ❖ A healthy heart is "whole." Integrated. Not splintered and broken.
- ❖ A healthy heart is full of positive expectation.
- ❖ When believers walk by faith and not sight, they anticipate the good God will do.
- ❖ Love is a wonderful gift from God. All believers have a deposit of love in their hearts. Love empowers believers' behavior.
- ❖ Like love, God has given believers peace and joy.
- ❖ Who wouldn't be exuberantly happy knowing the Creator of the whole universe is your Father.
- ❖ When believers know the true nature of God (e.g., He is sovereign, merciful, forgiving, and able to heal, deliver, rescue, and provide), their hearts can fill with hope.
- ❖ Hope has a stabilizing force on believers' minds. The assurance of knowing everything will be OK is priceless.
- ❖ Today, God directly gives believers wisdom in their hearts by the Holy Spirit.
- ❖ A healthy heart is soft and tender.

CHAPTER 31 STUDY QUESTIONS
Qualities of a Healthy Heart

1. Describe the order of a healthy heart.

2. Name two conditions that might cause a believer's heart to not be whole.

3. Why would a believer's heart be full of positive expectation?

4. Can God fill believers' hearts with love, peace, and joy? Yes No

5. Will a healthy heart contain hope? Yes No

QUALITIES OF A HEALTHY HEART

6. What kind of wisdom would a healthy heart contain?

   _____
   _____
   _____
   _____

7. Describe a tender heart.

   _____
   _____
   _____
   _____

CHAPTER 32

Heart Worship

But the hour is coming, and now is, when the true worshipers will worship the Father in spirit and truth; for the Father is seeking such to worship Him. God is Spirit, and those who worship Him must worship in spirit and truth.
—John 4:23–24

Heart worship is the act of turning inward to reverence and honor God. John 4:24 says, "God is Spirit, and those who worship him must worship in spirit and in truth." If people are in the spirit, they are not in thoughts based on the senses. In the spirit is being where God is. God is not in the shallows. He is found in the deep recesses of the heart. The prayer posture of hands together in front of a person symbolizes the meeting place with God. It is in the heart.

Consider the Tabernacle in the Old Testament. God's presence was neither in the outer courts where the altar of sacrifice and laver were erected nor where the showbread, golden candlestick, or incense altar rested. God's presence was in the innermost room over the mercy seat. The inner sanctuary was called the Holy of Holies. It's hard to imagine the Creator of the universe in such a small place. In the New Testament, God's presence is everywhere by His Spirit but is also in another confined area. Believers' hearts are the present–day Holy of Holies.

HEART WORSHIP

In the Holy of Holies, the High Priest could not approach God any old way. He had to wash, wear designated apparel, and come on a particular day with an offering of blood. Nadab and Abihu, the sons of Aaron, approached God in an unauthorized way and were consumed by fire (Leviticus 10:1–3: "Then Nadab and Abihu, the sons of Aaron, each took his censer and put fire in it, put incense on it, and offered profane fire before the LORD, which He had not commanded them. So fire went out from the LORD and devoured them, and they died before the LORD. And Moses said to Aaron, 'This is what the LORD spoke, saying: By those who come near Me I must be regarded as holy; and before all the people I must be glorified' So Aaron held his peace."). There is an inappropriate way to approach God.

The word "worship" in John 4:24 is "proskuneo," meaning to willingly kiss the ground while putting oneself in a humble and submissive position. It also means adoring while on one's knees with outstretched hands. Heart worship assumes an inward stance of humility before our God and King. A person may choose to bow to God outwardly as well. Worshiping God also involves God's Word. John 4:24 says, "...those who worship Him [God] must worship in spirit and in truth." John 6:63 says, "It is the Spirit who gives life; the flesh profits nothing. The words that I speak to you are spirit, and they are life." The more believers read the Word, the more profoundly and intimately they can respect and reverence God.

Prayer Point: Father, help me to turn away from this world, and to turn inward so that I may reverently worship and honor Your presence within me.

CHAPTER 32 KEY POINTS
Heart Worship

- ❖ Heart worship is the act of turning inward with the purpose of reverencing and honoring God.
- ❖ In the spirit is being where God is. God is not in the shallows. He is found in the deep recesses of the heart.
- ❖ The prayer posture of hands together in front of a person symbolizes the meeting place with God. It is in the heart.
- ❖ In the Tabernacle, God's presence was in the innermost room over the mercy seat.
- ❖ It's hard to imagine the Creator of the universe in such a small place.
- ❖ Believers' hearts are the present–day Holy of Holies.
- ❖ In the Holy of Holies, the High Priest could not approach God any old way.
- ❖ There is an inappropriate way of approaching God.
- ❖ The word "worship" in John 4:24 is "proskuneo," meaning to willingly kiss the ground while putting oneself in a humble and submissive position. It also means adoring while on one's knees with outstretched hands.
- ❖ Heart worship is assuming an inward stance of humility before our God and King.
- ❖ Worshiping God also involves God's Word.
- ❖ The more believers read the Word, the more deeply and intimately they can respect and reverence God.

CHAPTER 32 STUDY QUESTIONS
Heart Worship

1. Describe heart worship.

2. Describe the layout of the Old Testament tabernacle.

3. What is the Holy of Holies?

4. Where do believers meet with God?

5. Write out John 4:23–24.

6. What is God seeking for in John 4:23–24.

7. What could you do to improve your heart worship?

CHAPTER 33

Heart Song

And so it was, when the spirit from God was upon Saul, that David would take a harp and play it with his hand. Then Saul would become refreshed and well, and the distressing spirit would depart from him.
—1 Samuel 16:23

Music is such a wonderful part of life. It has such great power. Have you ever played a favorite praise and worship song and felt a lift in your spirit, soul, and body? Consider what happened when David played music for Saul. First Samuel 16:23 says Saul would become "refreshed and well." Certain music can have delivering and healing properties.

A heart song is a tune that comes from deep within. It doesn't originate in the mind. It's not something a person is thinking about or conjuring up. It's playing in the spirit. God can give a person a song. Psalm 40:3 says, "He has put a new song in my mouth – Praise to our God; many will see it and fear, and will trust in the Lord." Where did this song come from? If you read verses 1 and 2, it appears this song came from having gone through a difficult life situation with God's help. (Psalm 40:1–2: "I waited patiently for the LORD and He inclined to me, and heard my cry. He also brought me up out of a horrible pit, out of the miry clay, and set my feet upon a rock, and established my steps.")

I remember a person who went through a medical crisis. First, one tumor was found, and then three more. The man prayed and felt led to go to a well–known medical center in another city. He underwent more scans and waited. In the meantime, he served in the soup kitchen in that area and spent time with people experiencing homelessness. After five days, he received a phone call that his most recent scans were completely clear of tumors. He was healed. He went to a Christian meeting later that day and, out of the blue, was asked if he wanted to sing a song. He thought for a few seconds, having had no preparation, and immediately felt inspired to sing about what he had just gone through. He started softly about the worry and uncertainty he had just been through and ended loudly singing the praises of God, who he knows healed him.

A heart song can have tremendous power, especially when it contains a testimony (Revelation 12:11: "And they overcame him by the blood of the Lamb and by the word of their testimony, and they did not love their lives to the death."). Testimonies are spiritual weapons. No one can argue with someone's personal experience. When someone talks about what God did, it can sabotage the enemy's plans to keep people in sin, lies, and bondage.

People can wake up with a song on their heart. God typically sends a heart song for a reason. Honoring what is deposited in the heart is essential. When I've received heart songs, I try to write them down and usually start singing them out loud. I pay close attention to the words and meditate on the meaning. Songs are messages. It's a good idea to ask God what He's trying to communicate or do through the song. Sometimes, a heart song is for warfare. Other times, God is declaring what He is going to do. The words may be Scripture verses and may directly attack the enemy. The words may need to be spoken so the angels can hear and fulfill them.

Another type of heart song is making a melody in your heart to the Lord. Ephesians 5:19 says, "Speaking to one another in psalms and hymns and spiritual songs, singing and making melody in your heart to the Lord." One can intentionally sing songs to God, praising His greatness and virtues. This is a great way to spend time with the Lord.

Sometimes, the song in your heart is brand new to you. I remember receiving songs in my heart a few years into my Christian walk. I was amazed because the words came with a melody, almost like the whole song was deposited inside my spirit as a package. Here's a heart song about growing in my relationship with Jesus:

> *Jesus is my light and love.*
> *A precious gift from above.*
> *Thank you, Father, dear.*
> *I have no more fear.*
> *Jesus has received me.*
> *We are one, we are one.*
> *Our life has just begun.*
> *Jesus and me.*
> *Jesus and me.*
> *Jesus and me.*

Here's a short heart song I received during a time of decentralization, shifting, and reprioritizing:

> *Turn and shine.*
> *Turn and shine.*
> *Live a life of God's design.*
> *Turn and shine.*
> *Turn and shine.*
> *Look to Him.*
> *Turn and shine.*

Here's a heart song I received about evangelism:

> *Mining the earth*
> *There are souls in there to birth*
> *Let's go to the task*
> *For the fruit will not last.*
> *Let's mine the earth.*
> *Let's not give up the fight*
> *Working day and night.*
> *To gather what was sowed*
> *And wave it before the Lord.*
> *Let's mine the earth.*

Next time you have a song in your heart, don't ignore it. It could be sent from God for a specific purpose. Please write it down. Keep it in front of you. Sing it with all your heart. Watch God use it mightily for your good and His glory!

Prayer Point: Father, make me aware of the songs You put on my heart and reveal their purpose.

CHAPTER 33 KEY POINTS
Heart Song

- A heart song is a tune that comes from deep within. It doesn't originate in the mind.
- God can give a person a song.
- Psalm 40:3 says, "He has put a new song in my mouth – Praise to our God; many will see it and fear, and will trust in the Lord."
- A heart song can have tremendous power, especially when it contains a testimony.
- Testimonies are spiritual weapons.
- When someone talks about what God did, it can sabotage the enemy's plans to keep people in sin, lies, and bondage.
- People can wake up with a song on their heart.
- God typically sends a heart song for a reason.
- Honoring what is deposited in the heart is important.
- Songs are messages. It's a good idea to ask God what He's trying to communicate or do through the song.
- Sometimes a heart song is for warfare. Other times God is declaring what He is going to do.
- Another type of heart song is making melody in your heart to the Lord.
- Ephesians 5:19 says, "Speaking to one another in psalms and hymns and spiritual songs, singing and making melody in your heart to the Lord."
- One can intentionally sing songs to God praising His greatness and virtues. This is a great way to spend time with the Lord.
- Sometimes the song in your heart is brand new to you.
- Next time you have a song in your heart, don't ignore it. It could be sent from God for a specific purpose.

CHAPTER 33 STUDY QUESTIONS
Heart Song

1. What is a heart song?

2. Write out Psalm 40:3 and explain what it means.

3. Can believers wake up with a song on their heart? Yes No

4. Can songs on the heart be messages from God? Yes No

5. Can heart songs be used in spiritual warfare? Yes No

6. Write out Ephesians 5:19.

7. Can people make melodies in their heart to the Lord? Yes No

Made in United States
North Haven, CT
16 September 2024